D1526425

The Pedestrian Pocket Book
A NEW SUBURBAN DESIGN STRATEGY

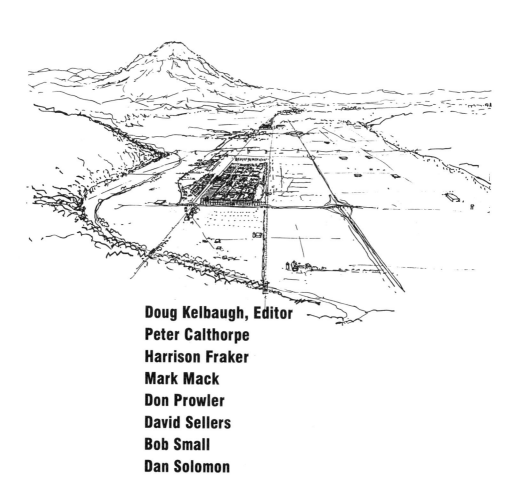

Doug Kelbaugh, Editor
Peter Calthorpe
Harrison Fraker
Mark Mack
Don Prowler
David Sellers
Bob Small
Dan Solomon

Princeton Architectural Press
IN ASSOCIATION WITH THE UNIVERSITY OF WASHINGTON

Published by
Princeton Architectural Press
37 East Seventh Street
New York, NY 10003
212.995.9620

Editor: Amy S. Weisser.
Special thanks to Sheila Cohen, Clare Jacobson,
Kevin C. Lippert, Elizabeth Short, Ann C. Urban.
Photo Credits: Amon Carter Museum, Fort Worth, Texas, pp.
22, 23; Da Capo Press, p. 26; Fondation LeCorbusier, p. 28;
Philip Morris, U.S.A., p. 25.

Library of Congress Cataloguing-in-Publication Data
The Pedestrian pocket book.
    1. Planned communities—Congresses. 2. Suburbs—Plan-
ning—Case studies—Congresses. 3. Planned communities—
Washington (State)—Auburn—Case Studies—Congresses.
I. Kelbaugh, Doug.
HT169.55.P44 1989   307.1'214   89–10500
ISBN 0–910413–68–1

This book is dedicated to Casey and Tess, for whom the charrette came at a very trying time in their family life and who are, alas, no longer part of the twenty-seven percent.

Pre-Charrette Press Release

March 1988, Seattle, Washington — The Department of Architecture at the University of Washington will be hosting a design charrette during the week of March 28 to April 1. This intensive workshop will team architecture students with eight distinguished architects. Together they will explore and apply a new suburban development strategy called "The Pedestrian Pocket," a concept that combines light rail transit, computerized back offices, low-rise apartment housing, and a mixed-use Main Street. The strategy will be tested on a site in Auburn, next to a proposed rapid transit line. The guest team leaders will be Dan Solomon, Mark Mack and Peter Calthorpe of San Francisco and the University of California at Berkeley, Harrison Fraker of Minneapolis (University of Minnesota), Don Prowler of Philadelphia (University of Pennsylvania), David Sellers of Vermont (formerly Yale University), all of whom are renowned practitioners as well as professors. They will be joined by Professors Robert Small and Doug Kelbaugh of the University of Washington.

Contents

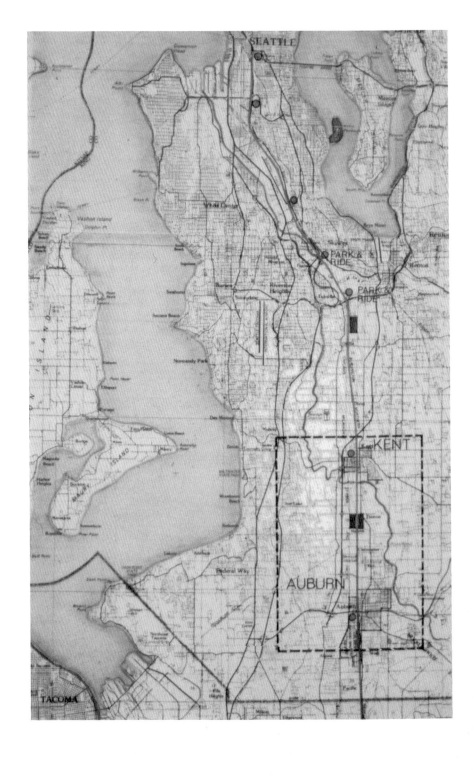

Preface

Of the seventeen million new households to be formed in the 1980s, it was estimated that 51 percent would be composed of single persons—including the elderly—or individuals unrelated to each other, that 22 percent would be single-parent families, and that only 27 percent would contain married couples. *Only 27 percent would contain married couples!* This astonishing prediction made by the United States Census Bureau in 1979 signaled one of the profound demographic changes for America in the latter half of the twentieth century. The nuclear family, for whom suburbia was conceived, now represents barely one out of four new households. "But we are still building World War II suburbs as if families were large and had only one breadwinner, as if jobs were all downtown, as if land and energy were endless, and as if another lane on the freeway would end traffic congestion." With this simple but irrefutable diatribe, Peter Calthorpe starts his essay on Pedestrian Pockets, a new suburban development strategy. These observations, embarrassing in their obviousness, have galvanized a band of architects/urban designers. Tiring of the dogmatic if convincing urban design theories of Krier and witnessing softer energy prices delay and deflect the energy and environmental movement, some of us have turned to *The Suburban Project*.

This new embrace is not meant to discount recent urban design theory, which has made a welcome about-face in the last ten years. The shift from the inventive object building of modernism to the recent interest in typological convention, in the "background building," and in historical and spatial continuity and contiguity has been a valuable lesson from Europe. (This present is a late but appreciated repayment for the Marshall Plan, which ironically exported some naive and devastating notions of urban renewal embedded in its economic package.) Nor is the suburban project intended to devalue the environmental and energy victories of the last two decades. For example, the shift from the standardization and mass production of modernism to site-specific and climate-conscious design has been a major positive legacy of the passive solar movement of the 1970s and of critical regionalism of the 1980s. It is now safe to say that most of the theoretical problems of urban design and the technical problems of energy conservation have been addressed. New, mature paradigms have already emerged and been adopted. What remains is primarily the hard work of implementing these paradigms. We do not need to focus on new typologies for urban design—2000 years have shown us well enough how to build livable *cities*.

What we desperately need are new, compelling typologies for our *suburbs*—ones that take the low-density, homogenous net that has been thrown over the outskirts of our cities and gather it into finite knots—bounded, contained, lively, and pedestrian communities. The old model of the single-family dwelling, large lawn, garage, swimming pool, curving cul-de-sac, and automobile commute to school, office park, shopping center, and recreation still holds sway in the minds of many planners, developers and design professionals, not to mention in the dreams of many home buyers.

A relatively idealistic, occasionally utopian group of architects have coalesced around this study. We have all been committed—at one time or another—to advocacy planning and energy-conscious design, by and large eschewing conventional architectural careers. We see the urbanization of suburbia as one of the next clarion calls for architects and planners to answer, even to rally around. Ironically, after years of bad-mouthing the suburban environment in which most of us grew up, we want to turn our attention toward bringing more physical structure and more metaphysical meaning to this placeless smear called the suburbs. The hard-won fruits of recent urban and ecological victories must of course be defended. But at the same moment the vast and seemingly inexorable process of suburbanization must be challenged, even though it seems so inevitable, so inexhaustible and so hopelessly far gone—a little like nuclear power once appeared and nuclear arsenals still seem. Most design professionals think that society is simply stuck with endless suburbs, but the authors of this booklet are convinced a transformation can be made.

This little book shows that strategic interventions could affect a remarkable change on suburbia; that structure, legibility and a sense of place are still possible, that finite centers of community are achievable, and that affordability, traffic decongestion, open space, mixed population, and mixed use are all mutually compatible. This is a tall order for a design strategy and may sound overly optimistic and shop-worn at the same time. We don't think so.

The search is for nothing less than a new American dream—one that restores public life to our communities, that trades half its 10,000 miles of automobile trips per person per year for light rail and exchanges television and computers for face-to-face communication, that recovers the mixed use of Main Street, that delivers true pedestrian accessibility, that again promises the pleasures of the high-speed mobility and expedition of our incredible freeway system, and that preserves the open countryside and farmland which provide emotional and physical sustenance and relief to city dwellers and serve as the lungs and liver for the congested cities. We are not very smitten with Deconstructionism, which seems more interested in accepting, expressing and even celebrating the alienating fragmentation, the disorder and the acuteness of modern life. Nor is our search much concerned with the tragic and unpopulated, if hauntingly beautiful, renditions of public space and abstract monuments of neo-rationalism. Indeed, the Pedestrian Pocket is an optimistic attempt to repair and restore a healthy sense of community and civic sanity. It was with this ambitious, even quixotic, agenda that a group of us convened a one week design workshop, or "charrette," in the parlance of design professionals. The charrette was held during the spring of 1988 in Seattle at the University of Washington. If this opening rhetoric attempts to answer why we are committed to the ideas in this book, the following ones try to explain the who, what, where, and when of its contents.

First, what exactly is a Pedestrian Pocket? A Pedestrian Pocket is "a simple cluster of housing, retail space and offices within a quarter-mile walking radius of a transit system." It represents a suburban development strategy that utilizes several proven architectural and urban typologies, none of which in and of themselves are particularly new or innovative—except when taken in combination. In the aggregate, these strategies

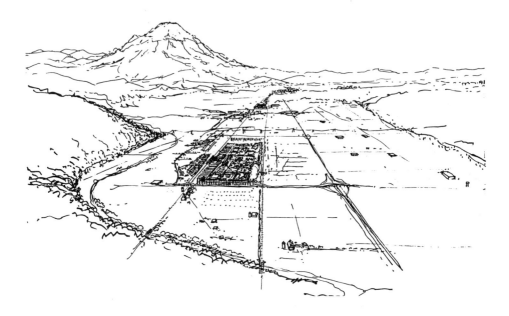

Aerial view of the Calthorpe/ Kelbaugh scheme, showing how miniscule an event a Pedestrian Pocket is in the landscape in comparison to the Green River valley in which it sits or to Mount Rainier in the distance.

take on compelling power. The four key concepts are low-rise, high-density housing, mixed-use "Main Street," light rail transit, and either the regional shopping mall or the computerized "back office." A Pedestrian Pocket is a straightforward confluence of land and transportation planning, affordable housing and contemporary (if questionable) notions of shopping and computerized commerce—all set within a short walk of a commuter rail station that links the Pedestrian Pocket to existing residential, commercial, educational, and recreational centers, as well as to other Pockets.

There are significant differences between Pedestrian Pockets (PPs) and both New Towns and Planned Unit Developments (PUDs). PPs are one-tenth the size of many New Towns. This smaller scale alone makes PPs more feasible and less disruptive. And their richer mix of uses and building types make them more comprehensive and heterogeneous than PUDs. There are less significant differences with the Traditional Neighborhood Development—a suburban design strategy now being crafted on the East Coast by Duany and Plater-Zyberk— an approach that is sympathetic in intent to Pedestrian Pockets and which represents, along with their Seaside, Florida town plan, a quantum leap forward in contemporary American suburbs.

x

How a Pedestrian Pocket translates into specific physical form is the subject of this book, although the text and the e-vents leading up to it are the first, admittedly raw, attempts to apply the development strategy to a real site. *The Pedestrian Pocket Book* is the recapitulation of an intensive design work-shop and the articles, lectures and reviews that the brief week of design produced. It is not meant to be a polished or defini-tive presentation of the idea but rather an early salvo in the war for suburbia.

The site of Auburn, Washington was selected for testing the hypothesis. Auburn is a town of approximately 30,000 people, located 24 miles south of downtown Seattle, in the flat plain of the Green River Valley. It is a working town, with a large Boeing plant, an early twentieth-century downtown, several shopping strips, an airport, and a broad valley floor that has been converted from truck farms to truck warehouses. This fer-tile, cheap, flat valley—served by rail and freeway—is ripe for light industrial development; Pedestrian Pockets can both help to preserve it and to put it to better use. The zone resembles a great deal of suburban and ex-urban agricultural land that is being gobbled up, often for the lowest and worst uses, like the over-sized tilt-up concrete regional distribution centers used by retail chains. The site—a rectangle of slightly over a half mile in length and approximately ninety acres of area—is squeezed between two north-south rail lines a quarter mile apart. This site was selected because one of these lines is proposed for a new rapid transit system between Seattle and Tacoma. The land, poorly drained and very flat, remains undeveloped, ex-cept for a dilapidated farm in the northeast corner. It is roughly three miles north of Auburn's town center; another three miles up the track stands Kent, a city of similar size and character. Distinguishing features of the site include the noise of the freight trains that roll past each flank dozens of times a day and, happily, an open view of Mt. Rainier. Rising from practical-ly sea level to its glaciated peak of 14,500 feet, this mountain is arguably the country's most dramatic and beautiful. Its magic helps to pull the site, on clear days anyway, out of its feature-less ordinariness.

The main players in this project are the eight team leaders and the sixty students who labored with them. The team leaders worked in pairs: Mark Mack and Don Prowler, Dave Sellers and Bob Small, Dan Solomon and Harrison Fraker, Peter

Calthorpe and myself. All are practicing architects with an interest in urbanism. In addition, all teach or have taught in architectural schools, such as Berkeley, Yale and the Universities of Pennsylvania, Washington and Minnesota. Many have worked together on other design charrettes: one such design workshop, on sustainable communities, took place in 1980 at Westerback Ranch, and another, on the urban river front, was held in 1987 in Turin, Italy. The undergraduate and graduate students who participated were all in their final years at the University of Washington Department of Architecture.

Before acknowledging the other people who helped make this booklet possible, let me briefly walk you through its contents. Following this preface are two essays by Peter Calthorpe. The first is a very short one on what a Pedestrian Pocket is *not*; the second is the seminal article on what *it is*. Dan Solomon's lecture on suburbia, delivered during the charrette, follows; then comes the building program for the site. The core of the text are the four actual designs done during the charrette. The book concludes with selected comments from the public jury and a short news report published in *Progressive Architecture*, a journal which consistently lends editorial support to this and other emerging strategies for suburban development (for example, see the May 1989 editorial by Robert Geddes and the feature article edited by Tom Fisher).

Although this book is short, the list of supporting cast is long. Among the many contributors to our endeavor, the Director of Planning from the town of Auburn, Mary McCumber, who was assisted by Greg Fewins, provided invaluable assistance. Together, McCumber and Fewins helped identify the site for the project, supplied necessary information and shared their insights and knowledge about this town. We hope that a Pedestrian Pocket or some variation of it will someday be realized in Auburn. In any case, we are thankful for their cooperation.

Other participants in the charrette included the panelists who critiqued the work in a public review at the end of the week. Their names and some of their comments are given toward the end of the book. Chris Peragine was both a contributor and an editor of this publication, and Mark McIntire did the preliminary graphic design.

All of the above have our hearty appreciation. In addition, I am personally grateful to Professors Christian Staub and Richard Alden for photographing the results and to Toni

Franklin, Gail Creager and Joanne Hanley, all of the University of Washington Department of Architecture for their support in organizing and recording the event and its aftermath. Harrison Fraker, Dean of the School of Architecture and Landscape Architecture at the University of Minnesota, deserves thanks for underwriting his time and expenses for the charrette. Lois Schwennesen, Manager of King County's Planning and Community Development Division, warrants mention and gratitude for her moral support of this project, as does Milenko Matanovic for sharing his vision and enthusiasm with me. Thank you also to Princeton Architectural Press: to Kevin Lippert for his foresight in publishing such an embryonic effort and to Amy Weisser for editing a band of rag-tag writers.

The last but far from least acknowledgement must go to the students, who worked around-the-clock for five days—often thanklessly and at the beck and whim of their leaders. Although the *raison d'etre* of the Pedestrian Pocket Charrette was not ostensibly pedagogic, it is hoped that the students participating in the raw advancement and testing of an idea learned as much or more than in a standard studio. If nothing else, the participants received a taste of the fast pace and high pressure of contemporary practice and of how much time and ego must be given up for a successful team effort.

Academic charrettes provide an opportunity for universities to expand knowledge, as well as preserve and disseminate it. They are living design laboratories that are different from both research and classroom by virtue of their synergy and adrenaline. True, a charrette is short-lived, episodic and sometimes subject to fatal wrong turns or truncated thinking forced by a clock that ticks much faster than normal. But the chemistry of both collaboration with team-mates and competition between teams seems to always unleash ideas that would otherwise remain overlooked in slower paced, more linear design methods. The confusion of a charrette—at times considerable—can give rise to fertile creativity. Of course the results of this quickened creativity must be widely and carefully reviewed. And the ideas must be reworked again and again by these and other players. *The Pedestrian Pocket Book* starts to do just that.

Doug Kelbaugh, FAIA
Seattle, Washington
May 1989

Drawings of the site by Art
Peterson, University of
Washington architecture
student.

Introduction
A REVERSE DEFINITION

PETER CALTHORPE

The current round of suburban growth is generating a crisis of many dimensions: mounting traffic congestion, increasingly unaffordable housing, receding open space, and stressful social patterns. The truth is, we are using planning strategies that are forty years old and no longer relevant to today's culture. Our household makeup has changed dramatically, the work place and work force have been transformed, real wealth has shrunk, and serious environmental concerns have surfaced. But we are still building World War II suburbs as if families were large and had only one breadwinner, as if jobs were all downtown, as if land and energy were endless, and as if another lane on the freeway would end congestion.

This is a proposal for an alternate suburban pattern of growth, the Pedestrian Pocket. The Pedestrian Pocket is a simple cluster of housing, retail space and offices within a quarter-mile walking radius of a transit system. The concept blends the convenience of the car and the opportunity to walk in an environment in which the economic engine of new growth—jobs in the service and information industry—is balanced with affordable housing and local stores. It is a planning strategy that preserves open space and re-duces automobile traffic without increasing density in existing neighborhoods. By its mix, the Pedestrian Pocket allows people a choice of walking, driving, carpooling, or riding mass transit. With new light rail lines, roads dedicated to car pools and buses and a corresponding upzoning of each of its stations, these Pockets re-connect an existing suburban fabric and its towns. The increments of growth are small, but the whole system accommodates regional expansion with minimal environmental impact: less land con-sumed, less traffic generated, and less pollution produced.

 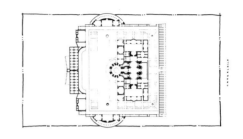

Medieval town of Carcasonne and ancient Roman monument, the Baths of Caracalla, super-imposed on Pedestrian Pocket site. The size of the Pedestrian Pocket is small, based on the scale of the human body rather than the scale of the automobile, and embraces a small increment of growth.

The Pedestrian Pocket is a concept for some new growth; it is not intended to displace urban renewal efforts, and it will certainly not totally eclipse suburban sprawl. It will, however, extend the range of choices available to the family buying a home, the business seeking relocation, the environmentalist hoping to preserve open space, and the existing community attempting to balance the benefits and liabilities of growth.

The Pedestrian Pocket is not a New Town. New Towns are typically much larger mixed-use complexes designed to be in-dependent of the surrounding developments and towns. The garden cities movement in England posited New Towns of approximately 30,000 people. The original Garden City, Letchworth, was to have 20,000 people on 3,800 acres. Found throughout Europe today New Towns contain a full range of jobs, housing and services and, as in Milton Keynes in England, accommodate up to 350,000 people on 22,000 acres. The Pe-destrian Pocket, on the other hand, houses approximately 5,000 people with jobs for 3,000 on no more than 100 acres—the area within walking distance of a transit station.

In the United States, New Towns have proved to be financial-ly too demanding for private sector developers. The massive cost of infrastructure and its long gestation period drives New Town costs beyond the staying capacity of non-public institu-tions. The fates of Reston and Columbia exemplify the financial hardship of such massive undertakings. Reston, which can be considered successful at this time, has been through several ownerships in its twenty-year history; each succeeding owner comes closer to a stage of development that balances invest-ment with return. Centralized governments, such as Sweden's, have a greater degree of success in planning and executing New Towns because of their financial durability and market control. But political will and long-term policy stability are essential for undertakings of this scale and duration.

In contrast the Pedestrian Pocket grows at an increment typical of current market-place activities; one hundred-acre projects are common for sub-divisions, office parks and shopping centers. Although more complex than these single-use types, the Pedestrian Pocket never gets too far ahead of market demand or creates massive front-end infrastructure costs. Similarly the political will to plan for a Pedestrian Pocket does not carry the burden of extensive public financing or taxes. Nor does it involve the "social engineering" associated with New Towns. The public sector merely zones for a broad cross section of uses within the transit area and allows the market forces to determine what should be built and when.

Beyond the simple economic and political problems of New Towns lies this other difficult trait: their isolation and lack of history. By their very independence they cut themselves off from the historical evolution of a region, its complexity and its diversity. Although their execution may take several decades, they are necessarily stand-alone projects with a more uniform architecture and aesthetic than places that have evolved over longer periods of time. Some attempts have been made to integrate existing villages into larger New Towns, but the desired communication is rarely achieved. Many people find New Towns sterile and heartless, no matter how efficient and convenient they may be.

By implanting small clusters of new development within the existing metropolis, Pedestrian Pockets avoid the isolation and "newness" of New Towns. A Pedestrian Pocket does not function as a self-sufficient town. People are not expected to work in the same Pocket in which they live or to find all their shopping needs or recreation within the hundred-acre development. In fact, the Pockets are meant to weave back together the currently isolated parts of our suburban environment; to put the elderly and kids without cars within reach of old downtowns as well as new shopping malls, parks and other Pockets; to allow workers access to existing and new job opportunities throughout a transit region, not just within a single town. Pedestrian Pockets are intended to balance growth in a developed region, enhancing and extending the diversity, complexity and history of the area. As is true in the modern suburb, in a Pedestrian Pocket people would come to see themselves as citizens of the larger region rather than as participants in the fiction of an isolated town or city.

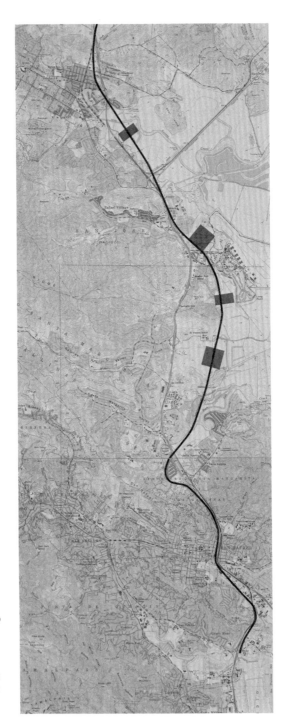

An example of Pedestrian Pocket growth projected for Marin County in California. The map shows an abandoned railroad right-of-way which can be converted into a light rail system connecting the new growth with existing major towns and a ferry to San Francisco. The four Pockets shown to scale would accommodate fifteen years of the county's projected growth.

Pedestrian Pockets
NEW STRATEGIES FOR SUBURBAN GROWTH

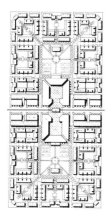

Generic diagram for a 60-acre Pedestrian Pocket.

PETER CALTHORPE

There is a profound mismatch between the old suburban patterns of settlement we have evolved since World War II and the post-industrial culture in which we now find ourselves. This mismatch is generating traffic congestion, a dearth of affordable and appropriate housing, environmental stress, a loss of open space, and lifestyles that burden working families and isolate the elderly and singles living alone. This mismatch has two primary sources: a dramatic shift in the nature and location of our work place and a fundamental deviation in the character of our increasingly diverse households.

Traffic congestion in the suburbs signals a strong change in the structure of our culture. The computer and service industries have led to the decentralization of the work place, causing new traffic patterns and "suburban gridlock." Where downtown employment once dominated, suburb-to-suburb traffic now produces greater commuting distances and time. Throughout the country, over forty percent of all commuting trips are now between suburbs. These new patterns have seriously eroded the quality of life in formerly quiet suburban towns. In the San Francisco Bay area, for example, 212 of the region's 812 miles of suburban freeway are regularly backed up during rush hours. That figure is projected to double within the next twelve years. As a result, recent polls have traffic continually heading the list as the primary regional problem, with the difficulty of finding good affordable housing running a close second.

Home ownership has become a troublesome—if not unattainable—goal, even with our double-income families. Affordable housing grows ever more elusive, and families have had to move to less expensive but more peripheral sites, consuming

Housing and commercial space border a central park leading to the light rail station. The park combines facilities for all age groups and doubles as an auto-free path to the station.

irreplaceable agricultural land and overloading roads. In 1970 about half of all families could meet the expense of a median-priced single-family home; today less than a quarter can.

Moreover, the basic criteria for housing have changed dramatically as single occupants, single parents, the elderly, and small double-income families redefine the traditional home. Our old suburbs were designed around a stereotypical household which is no longer prevalent. Over seventy-three percent of the new households in the 1980s lack at least one component of the traditional husband, wife and children model. Elderly people over 65 make up 23 percent of the total number of new homeowners, and single parents represent an astonishing twenty percent. Certainly the traditional three bedroom, single-family residence is relevant to a decreasing segment of the population. The suburban dream becomes even more complicated when one considers the problem of affordability.

In addition to these dominant questions of traffic and housing, longer range consequences of pollution, air quality, open-space preservation, the conversion of prime agricultural land, and growing infrastructure costs add to the crisis of post-industrial sprawl. These issues are manifested in a growing sense of frustration—placelessness—with the fractured quality of our

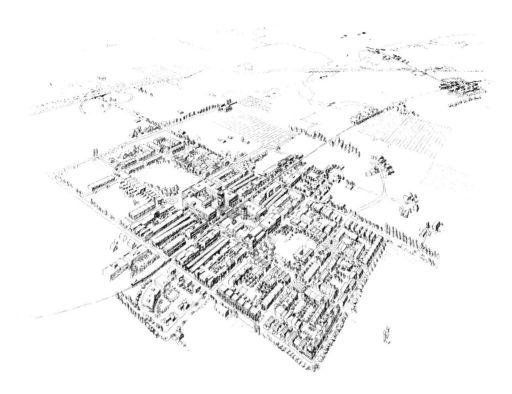

Balancing and clustering jobs, housing, shopping, recreation, and child care, the Pedestrian Pocket uses one-sixteenth the land area of a typical suburban development. Open space and precious agricultural land coexist with a region's growth.

suburban megacenters. The unique qualities of place are continually consumed by chain-store architecture, scaleless office parks and monotonous subdivisions.

THE SERVICE ECONOMY *DRIVING DECENTRALIZATION*

As new jobs have shifted from blue collar to white and grey, the computer has allowed the decentralization of the new service industries into mammoth low-rise office parks on inexpensive and often remote sites. The shift is dramatic: from 1973 to 1985 five million blue-collar jobs were lost nationwide while the service and information fields gained from 82 to 110 million jobs. This translated directly into new office complexes, with 1.1 billion square feet of office space constructed. Nationwide, these complexes have moved outside the central cities, with the percentage of total office in the suburbs shifting from 25 percent in 1970 to 57 percent in 1984.

Central to this shift is a phenomenon called the "back office," the new sweat shop of the post-industrial economy. The

9

The light rail station area borders ground-floor retail and neighborhood services. The office courtyard and main street intersect in a plaza with limited automobile access.

typical back office is large, often with a single floor area of one to two acres. About eighty percent of its employees are clerical, twelve percent supervisory and only eight percent managerial. In a survey of criteria for back-office locations, forty-seven major Manhattan corporations ranked cost of space first, followed by the quality of the labor pool and site safety. These criteria lead directly to the suburbs where land is inexpensive, parking is easy, and (most importantly) the work force is supplemented by housewives—college-educated, poorly paid, non-unionized, and dependable.

This low-density office explosion has rejuvenated suburban growth just as urban "gentrification" has run its course. The young urban professional has recently made a family commitment and feels the draw of the suburbs. Most of the growth areas in the United States—office parks, shopping malls and single-family dwelling sub-divisions—have a suburban character. Although such growth continually seems to reach the limits of automobile congestion and building moratoriums, there are no readily available alternatives that will enrich the dialogue between growth and no-growth factions, between public benefit and private gain, between the environmentalist and the businessperson.

THE PEDESTRIAN POCKET *A POST-INDUSTRIAL SUBURB*

Single-function, land-use zoning at a scale and density that eliminates the pedestrian has been the norm for so long that Americans have forgotten that walking can be part of their daily lives. Certainly, the present suburban environment is not walkable, much to the detriment of children, their chauffeur parents, the elderly, and the general health of the population. Urban redevelopment is a strong and compelling alternative to the suburban world but does not seem to fit the character or aspirations of major parts of our population and of many businesses. Mixed-use New Towns are no alternative, as the political consensus needed to back the massive infrastructure investments is lacking. By default, growth is directed mainly by the location of new freeway systems, the economic strength of the region and standard single-use zoning practices. Environmental and local opposition to growth only seems to spread the problem, either transferring the congestion to the next county or creating lower and more auto-dependent densities.

Much smaller than a New Town, the Pedestrian Pocket is defined as a balanced, mixed-use area within a quarter-mile or a five minute walking radius of a transit station. The functions within this 50 to 100-acre zone include housing, offices, retail, day care, recreation, and parks. Up to two thousand units of housing and one million square feet of office space can be located within three blocks of the transit station using typical residential densities and four-story office configurations.

The Pedestrian Pocket accommodates the car as well as transit and walking. Parking is provided for all housing and commercial space. The housing types are standard low-rise, high-density forms such as three-story walk-up apartments and two-story townhouses. Only the interrelationships and adjacent land use has changed. People have a choice: walk to work or to stores within the Pedestrian Pocket; take the light rail to work or to shop at another station; car pool on a dedicated right-of-way; drive on crowded freeways. In a small Pedestrian Pocket, homes are within walking distance of a neighborhood shopping center, several three-acre parks, day care, various services, and two thousand jobs. Within four stops of the light rail in either direction (ten minutes), employment is available for 16,000, or the amount of back-office growth equivalent to that of one of the nation's highest-growth suburbs over the last five years.

This mix of uses supports a variety of transportation means: walking, bus, light rail, car pool, and standard automobile. The goal is to create an environment that offers choices. Providing comfortable mid-day pedestrian access to retail, services, recreation, and civic functions is essential in order to encourage people to car pool. Similarly, the location of the station, whether bus or rail, near home or work and the realistic opportunity to handle errands without a car is tied to an individual's decision to use mass transit. A Pocket configuration that allows easy access by car to all commercial and residential development maintains the freedom of choice. The result is the best of both worlds.

The Pedestrian Pocket is located on a dedicated right-of-way which evolves with the development. Rather than bearing the large cost of a complete rail system as an initial expense, this right-of-way facilitates mass transit by providing exclusively for car pools, van pools, bikes, and buses. As the cluster matures, transit investments are made for light rail in the developed right-of-way. But the growth of this land-use pattern is not dependent on this investment; the system is designed to support many modes of traffic and to phase light rail into place when the population is great enough to support it.

The Pedestrian Pocket system would eventually act in concert with new light rail lines, reinforcing ridership and connecting existing employment centers, towns and neighborhoods with new development. Light rail lines are currently under construction in many suburban environments, such as, in California alone, Sacramento, San Jose, San Diego, Long Beach, and Orange County. They emphasize the economies of using existing right-of-ways and a simpler, more cost-effective technology than heavy rail. In creating a line of Pedestrian Pockets, the public sector's role is merely to organize the transit system and set new zoning guidelines, leaving development to the private sector. Much of the cost of the transit line can be covered by assessing the property owners benefiting from the increased densities.

The light rails in current use provide primarily a park-and-ride system to connect low-density sprawl with downtown commercial areas. In contrast, the Pedestrian Pocket system is decentralized, linking many nodes of high-density housing with many commercial destinations. Peak-hour traffic is multidirectional, reducing congestion and making the system more efficient. Bus systems, along with car-pool systems, can tie into

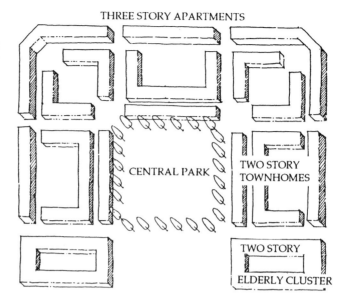

The Pedestrian Pocket provides for many types of housing needs: elderly clusters are at an easy stroll from park, services and trolley line; two-story townhouses with attached garages and private yards provide for families; three-story apartment buildings offer affordable housing for singles and childless couples.

THREE STORY APARTMENTS

CENTRAL PARK

TWO STORY TOWNHOMES

TWO STORY ELDERLY CLUSTER

the light rail. Several of the Pockets on a line have large parking facilities for park-and-ride access, allowing the existing suburban development to enjoy the services and opportunities of the Pockets. However, the location of the office, stores and services adjacent to the station and each other avoids the need for secondary mass transit or additional large parking areas.

The importance of the Pedestrian Pocket is that it provides balanced growth in jobs, housing and services, while creating a healthy mass-transit alternative for the existing community. The key lies in the form and mix of the Pocket. The pedestrian path system must be carefully designed and form a primary order for the place. If this is configured to allow the pedestrian comfortable and safe access, up to fifty percent of a household's typical automobile trips can be replaced by walking, car pool and light rail journeys. Not only does this produce a better living environment within the Pocket, but the reduction of traffic in the region is significant and in many cases essential.

HOUSING *DIVERSITY IN NEEDS AND MEANS*

Housing in the Pedestrian Pocket is planned to provide each of the primary household types with affordable homes that meet their needs. Families with children, single parents or couples need an environment in which kids can move safely, in which day care is integrated into the neighborhood, and in which commuting time is reduced. The townhouses and duplexes proposed for the Pedestrian Pocket allow these families to have all this as well as an attached garage, land ownership and a small private yard. These building types are more affordable to build and maintain than their detached counterparts yet still offer individual ownership and a private identity. The common open space, recreation, day care, and convenient shopping render these houses even more desirable. Group play areas are located off the townhouses' private yards and are connected to the central park and the commercial section by paths. One-third of the housing in a Pocket is of this type.

For singles and "empty-nesters," traditional two- and three-story apartment buildings or condominiums keep costs down while allowing access to the civic facilities, retail services and recreational amenities of the extended community. This segment of the population is traditionally more mobile and thus has an option of either rental or ownership housing. Elderly housing is located close to the parks, light rail and service retail; this eliminates some of the distance and alienation typical of housing facilities for the elderly. The housing is formed into courtyard clusters of two-story buildings which provide a private retreat area and the capacity for common facilities for dining and social activities. Residence in a pedestrian community allows the elderly to become a part of our everyday culture again and to enjoy the parks, stores and restaurants close at hand.

Several parks double as paths to the station area, a route which is pleasant and free of automobile crossings. The housing overlooking the parks provides security surveillance and twenty-four hour activity. Each Pocket offers a different arrangement of day-care buildings and general recreational facilities in its parks. Although the housing forms small clusters, the central park and facilities tend to unify the neighborhood, giving it an identity and commonality missing in most of our suburban tracts. An organization (much like a condominium home-owner's organization), which includes landlords, townhouse owners, tenants, office managers, and worker representatives, maintains the centers.

The goal of this tight mix of housing and open space is not just to provide more appropriate homes for the different users

The commercial center of the Pedestrian Pocket mixes large ground-floor retail, restaurants and smaller business. Retail faces the light rail line, and all employees are within walking distance of the station. Cars circulate on the shopping street and have access to parking structures.

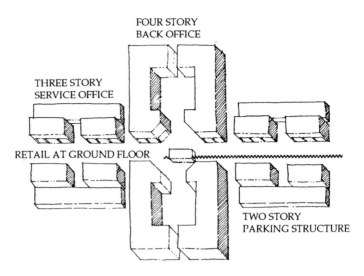

FOUR STORY
BACK OFFICE

THREE STORY
SERVICE OFFICE

RETAIL AT GROUND FLOOR

TWO STORY
PARKING STRUCTURE

or to offer the convenience of walking but hopefully to reintegrate the currently separated age and social groups of our diverse culture. The shared common spaces and local stores may create a rebirth of our lost sense of community and place.

COMMERCE AND COMMUNITY

Jobs are the fuel of new growth, of which the service and high-technology fields are the spearhead. For example, the San Francisco Bay region has currently about 63 percent of all its jobs in these areas. That percentage is expected to increase in the next twenty years, adding about 200,000 new jobs in high-technology and 370,000 new jobs in service. Retail activity and housing growth always follow in proportion to these primary income generators. The Pedestrian Pocket provides a framework that allows jobs and housing to grow in tandem.

The commercial buildings in the Pocket offer retail opportunities at their ground floor and offices above. The retail stores enjoy the local walk-in trade from offices and housing, as well as exposure to light rail and drive-in customers. All the stores face a "Main Street" on which the light rail line, the station and convenience parking for cars are mixed. This multiple exposure and access, along with the abundance of office workers, creates a strong market for the theaters, library, post office, food

15

The Pedestrian Pocket provides diverse open space: private yards for families, semi-public space for a group of houses, central parks to be used by all, and courtyards and a "Main Street" shopping area for the extended population. The central park offers a lunch place for workers, an after school playground for the kids, a site for shared day-care facilities, and an evening or weekend focus for the whole community. Walking paths connect the entire site without requiring the pedestrian to cross any streets.

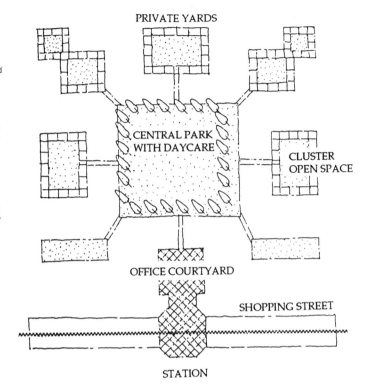

PRIVATE YARDS

CENTRAL PARK WITH DAYCARE

CLUSTER OPEN SPACE

OFFICE COURTYARD

SHOPPING STREET

STATION

stores, and other convenience stores located in the one hundred thousand square feet of retail.

The offices above the retail stores provide space for small entrepreneurial businesses, start-up firms and local community services. Behind these offices, parking structures capable of accommodating one-half the workers in all the commercial space are located. Presumably, the other half of the employees walk, car pool or arrive by light rail.

There is a 500,000 to 1,000,000 square foot potential in two to four office buildings per Pedestrian Pocket. These four-story buildings, with 60,000 square feet per floor, fit the size and cost criteria of most back-office employers. The buildings form a courtyard open to the station on one side and the park on the other. Office employees share day-care facilities and open space with the neighborhood.

The commercial mix attempts to balance housing with a desirable job market, stores, entertainment, and services. But

the commercial facilities and the offices are not entirely finan-
cially dependent on the local housing; access by automobile
from the existing neighborhoods and by light rail from other
Pockets augments the market. Similarly the transportation system makes a pool of employees available from a twenty-mile
range.

REGIONAL PLANNING AND THE PEDESTRIAN POCKET

Pedestrian Pockets are not meant to stand alone as developments; they are intended to form a network offering long-range
growth within a region. They will vary considerably given the
complexities of place and their internal makeup. Some may be
larger than the sixty-acre model we've been using as an example: the quarter-mile walking radius actually encloses 120
acres. Pockets may offer different focuses, with one providing a
regional shopping center, one—a cultural center, or a third—
housing and recreation. Some may be used as redevelopment
tools to provide economic incentives in a depressed area;
others may rejuvenate an aging shopping area; the remaining
Pockets may be located in new areas zoned for low-density
sprawl and in this way save much of the land from more dras-
tic development.

Pockets and their rail lines also connect to the existing as-
sets of an area. The system links the major towns, office parks,
shopping areas, and government facilities and allows those
from earlier communities to gain access to the Pocket system.
Many new light rail systems, built only to connect existing low-
density development, are experiencing some resistance from
people not wanting to leave their cars. The importance of re-
zoning for a comfortable walking distance from house to station
is to ease people out of their cars, to give them an alternative
which is convenient and pleasing. There is evidence that in
time such planning will succeed: In a study of San Francisco's
rail transit system, BART, it was discovered that fully forty percent of those who lived and worked within a five minute walk
of the station used the train to get to work.

To test this regional planning concept I chose an area north
of San Francisco, combining Marin and Sonoma counties.
Many consider the area prime turf for new post-industrial
sprawl. Sonoma is projected to have a 61 percent growth in
employment in the next twenty years, the highest in the Bay

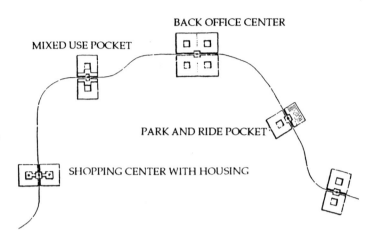

Pedestrian Pockets vary in use and size. Each Pocket is located about one mile from the next.

BACK OFFICE CENTER

MIXED USE POCKET

PARK AND RIDE POCKET

SHOPPING CENTER WITH HOUSING

region. Combined, these two counties are to grow by about 88,000 jobs and 63,000 households in the next 15 years. Of the new jobs, around 60,000 will be in the service, high-technology and knowledge fields, the equivalent of twenty million square feet of office and light industrial space. With standard planning techniques, this growth will consume massive quantities of open space and necessitate a major expansion of the freeway system. The result will still involve frustrating traffic jams.

Instead, twenty Pedestrian Pockets along a new light rail line accommodate this office growth with matching retail facilities, businesses and approximately thirty thousand new houses. Several additional pockets dedicated primarily to homes allow two-thirds of the area's housing demand to be met while linking the counties' main cities with a viable mass-transit system. A recently-acquired, Northwestern Pacific rail-road abandoned right-of-way, which would connect a San Francisco ferry terminal to the northernmost county seat, forms the spine for such a new pattern of growth.

SOCIAL AND ENVIRONMENTAL FORM

It is easy to talk quantitatively about the physical and environmental consequences of our new sprawl but very difficult to postulate their social implications. Many argue that there is no longer a casual relationship between the structure of our physical environment and that of our human well-being or social health. We are adaptable, they claim, and our communities form around interest groups and work rather than around any sense of place or group of individuals. Our center is abstract, not grounded in place, and our social forms are disconnected from home and neighborhood. Planners complicate the issue by polarizing urban and suburban forms. Some advocate a rigorous return to traditional city forms and almost pre-industrial culture, while others praise the evolution of the suburban megalopolis as the inevitable and desirable expression of our new technologies and hyper-individualized culture. However rationalized, these new forms have a restless and hollow feel, reinforcing our mobile state and the instability of our families. Moving at a speed that allows only generic symbols to be recognized, we cannot wonder that the man-made environment seems trite and overstated.

In proposing the Pedestrian Pocket the practical comes first; the Pedestrian Pocket preserves land, energy and resources, reduces traffic, renders homes more affordable, allows children and the elderly more access to services, and decreases commuting time for working people. The social consequences are less quantitative but perhaps equally compelling. They have to do with the quality of our shared world.

Mobility and privacy have increasingly displaced the traditional commons, which once provided the connected quality of our towns and cities. Our shared public space has been given over to the car and its accommodation, while our private world has become bloated and isolated. As our private world grows in breadth, our public world becomes more remote and impersonal. As a result, our public space lacks identity and is largely anonymous, while our private space strains toward a narcissistic autonomy. Our communities are zoned black or white, private or public, my space or nobody's. The automobile destroys the urban street, the shopping center destroys the neighborhood store, and the depersonalization of public space grows with the scale of government. Inversely, private space is taxed by the necessity of providing for many activities that were once shared and is further burdened by the need to create identity in a sea of monotony. Although the connection between such social issues and development is elusive and complex, it must be addressed by any serious theory of growth.

In one way, Pedestrian Pockets are utopian—they involve the directed choice of an ideal rather than of laissez-faire planning, and they make certain assumptions about social well-being. But by not assuming a transformation of our society or its people, they avoid the full label, and its subsequent pitfalls, of most utopian schemes. They represent instead a response to a transformation that has already expressed itself: the transformation from the industrial forms of segregation and centralization to the decentralized and integrated forms of the post-industrial era. And perhaps, Pedestrian Pockets express the positive environmental and social results of a culture adjusting itself to this new reality.

The use of different developers for each section assures architectural interest and diversity in the Pedestrian Pocket. Individuals can build their own townhouses, and housing cooperatives can develop clusters.

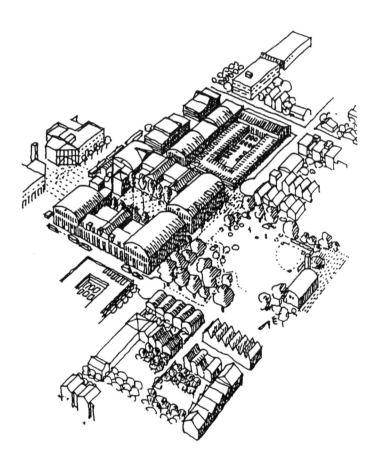

Fixing Suburbia

California, 1989. *Top*
Livermore, Ca., 1908. *Middle*
Livermore, 1981. *Bottom*

DANIEL SOLOMON

In the year 2000 the projected peak-hour average speed on the San Diego freeway from Los Angeles International Airport to Sunset Boulevard will be ten miles per hour. If one likes to keep track of disillusioning facts this could head one's list. It is more shattering to many people than anything to do with lust, greed, hypocrisy, violence, cruelty, or any of the other normal things that fill daily newspapers. It is more on the scale of the Ostrogoth's sack of Rome or the Fall of the Third Reich. It represents a point at which a complex of values that motivated the activities of a whole society collapses, a point at which ordinary people learn that in the future they must do what they have always done differently or not at all.

The illustration on the left is a 1908 United States Geological Survey map of a place called Livermore, California. It shows basically what all settlements in the western United States were like early in the century—a grid, which bends to follow the railroad, governs the boundaries of the farms as well as the gridiron town. Below is the same place in 1981. As you can clearly see sometime between the drawing of the two maps people changed their minds about how to live. An explosion of growth completely ignored both the agrarian grid and the gridiron town. The reason there is, I think, some interest in what we are doing [in the Pedestrian Pocket charrette] is that the majority of the electorate in places like the new wiggly parts of Livermore have suddenly realized that the world in which they live is profoundly screwed-up. They have come to see that it is the product of a set of dreams that are inherently self-nullifying; the more that is built according to these dreams, the less it is like what it was supposed to be.

Kuchel & Dresel, "Shasta, 1856, Shasta County, California," lithograph, 1856.

SHASTA. 1856.
SHASTA COUNTY, CALIFORNIA.
Published by A. Roman.

When life is less than perfect, people usually muddle through. For a long time suburban people have survived work days on 40,000 square feet floors in sealed skin buildings in office parks. They have survived the isolation and insularity of their dwellings; they have survived the disappearance of public life; they have survived pollution and the despoliation of the landscape. And they have gotten used to the shear ugliness of everything around them. Lots of people have learned not to mind that at all. But take away mobility, take away freedom, take away the great joy of driving—and there is big trouble. Comes gridlock; comes the revolution. There is then an angry horde, organized politically to fling itself in front of the juggernaut of growth and stop it dead. This is just now happening, and it makes this an important moment, a time for people involved in building to ask how our towns got to be such a mess—and what if anything can we do about it.

The whole evolution of the American townscape can be divided into two eras—one begins with the earliest colonial settlements and ends at a particular moment in 1938, and the other extends from 1938 to the present.

The first era of the American town commenced when the great agrarian grids were drawn across the continent: the 640-acre sections and six-mile square townships established by Congress in the East and Midwest and the Spanish land grants laid

22

E.S. Glover, "Bird's Eye View of Santa Barbara, California, 1877," lithograph, c. 1877.

out according to the Laws of The Indies in California and the Southwest. Roads followed section lines, and sections lines followed the compass—through swamps and over hilltops, a transcontinental triumph of the abstract over the particular. The builders of towns in the American West came with the idea of a town's makeup fully formed in their heads. It was an uninflected rationalist subdivision of the agrarian grid that served as an armature for the grafting of the urban culture of Europe onto the wilderness. The grid of San Francisco is as ruthless to its typography as the agrarian grids of the hinterlands were to lakes and forests.

These grids, combined with frontal, axial and typologically consistent buildings, made public spaces of streets and squares. Aldo Rossi said that the function of typology—invariant patterns in the organization of buildings—is to make the acts of individuals into the collective act of building and rebuilding the public space of towns. For a while, even well into the twentieth century, houses based upon the urbanism of the West were built in great numbers. The California bungalow, a house type that evolved in Southern California around 1910, became common all over the western United States and Canada. The bungalow is essentially an urban house. It is frontal and axial; it has a porch which is a semi-private zone between the rooms and the street; and its plan implies a street lined with porches and a town of porch-lined streets. It is a house with a town—a very nice, civilized town—implicit in its plan and its multiplication.

The second era of the American town was born on the day in 1938 when the Federal Housing Administration (FHA) began work on a national planning code. The residential planning begun by the FHA resulted in the FHA Minimum Property Standards (FHA-MPS), a document of incredible power which required observance of its planning guidelines as a condition for the receipt of Federal Mortgage insurance; this document substantially affected the vast explosion of post-war suburbia underwritten by the GI Bill. The polemic behind the FHA-MPS was that of Clarence Stein, Henry Wright and Charles Perry. The MPS was based on the belief that American gridiron towns could not accommodate the automobile. It imposed a pattern of enclaves rather than a continuous urban fabric; traffic was restricted to arterials, and houses stood on curving cul-de-sacs.

The second era of the American townscape took shape after World War II, and this second era is the condition in which we must live and work—at least those of us who reside on the West Coast.

The American town of the second era was brought about by two implacable forces of historic inevitability. The first is the victory of the private over the public. At the moment I am doing some work in Los Angeles, and when I go there I have a favorite hotel in Hollywood where I stay. Last time I was there, there was a flyer in my room for West Hollywood's newest cultural institution—the West Hollywood Wax Museum. According to the flyer the museum features life-like effigies of famous personalities such as Elvis, Jesus and Clint. It should not be surprising that in Hollywood, where they decide these things, Clint has achieved a status commensurate with the other two

and has earned the special honorific of no last name, like Peter, Philip, Michael, and Frank in the world of architecture. By some ways of reckoning Clint Eastwood is the perfect man. He is the private man *par excellence*. More than any other individual he is the repository and embodiment of the two mythologies that underlie most of what architects did for forty years, that motivated the housing industry in America and that were responsible for the great shift from the first era to the second era in American town building.

The first myth is the lone rider of the prairie. For people throughout the world, there has always been something compelling about the idea of Americans as a population that lives on the land, about the culture of vast distances that is so exotic and unattainable, so infinitely seductive to the masses of the industrial cities of Europe, England and the East Coast of the United States. That culture has been perpetuated, disseminated and made mythic by sixty years of cinema and by the real merchants of dreams—the advertising industry—for whom beer, cigarettes, cars, trucks, chewing gum, and clothing are the reification of the culture of the wilderness.

The lone rider of the prairie likes to be photographed on his horse, but he has to live somewhere, and American domestic architecture has long been involved in creating a habitat for him. Frank Lloyd Wright's houses in Oak Park were not called

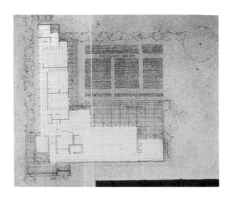

Frank Lloyd Wright, Usonian house, 1937.

"Oak Park Houses" or "houses on streets in a wealthy Chicago suburb," they were called "Prairie Houses." In the Prairie House, the protagonist is the lone rider who stands sheltered at his hearth, looks to the horizon and proclaims his ownership of whatever he sees. Space is omni-directional and private.

As the west became urbanized, the culture of the wilderness, not the town, prevailed. The Prairie House became the Usonian House. A Usonian House turns a blank face to the street, welcomes the automobile into the pattern of its plan and then explodes onto the land it claims as its own. Every feature of the Usonian House—the horizontality of details linking spaces one to another, the continuity of materials from inside to outside—states this claim: space is continuous in all directions.

In California the Usonian house, which had become the houses of Richard Neutra, in turn became the huge subdivisions of Joseph Elcher. The Usonian ideals of the Elcher houses were disseminated as necessary and inevitable by powerful journals like *Sunset* and *House & Garden*.

26

Usonian dwelling, à la
Richard Neutra.

Usonia realized.

The beauty of the Usonian house did not survive as a part of the American scene, but the house's skeleton did. The essential elements of the Usonian plan—the primacy of the automobile, the accessibility of the claimed prairie—are ideas that dominate American merchant houses in the 1980s. This banalized Usonian, stripped of its art, is a place where the town does not intercede between the freeway and the electric garage door; from the private car to the private landscape, there is no prospect of human encounter.

The universal dream of being the lone rider of the prairie is of course fundamentally anti-urban; the story of the West in the last forty years is a strange paradox—a period of intense urbanization based on images and aspirations that are non-urban. The anti-urbanity of the house of the lone rider is compacted by the automobile: the fact that the lone rider is able to trade his one horse for a mustang, a bronco and perhaps a boat, a boat trailer and a motorcycle or two.

The other myth that profoundly shaped our towns is the myth of the jock, a myth that Clint Eastwood also embodies.

Clint, Paul Newman and Robert Redford look the way they do in their late fifties because one of their principal activities and interests is taking care of themselves. It's not hard days on the Oregon Trail; it's nouvelle cuisine and exercise.

This obsession with vigor and fitness was of course foretold by the father of modernist urbanism, Le Corbusier, who proposed demolition of the urban culture of Europe in order to achieve it. His protagonist is the boxer, a fellow like Clint Eastwood. The boxer lives in a chaste white apartment with a few sticks of Corb furniture and stares out at a jungle—what Tony Vidler calls "jogging utopia." Corbu's vision was realized all over the place at the expense of main street and hometown, …but that of course is an old story.

So the great historic force that dismantled the American town of the first era is the triumph of the private as represented by the cowboy—with his cars—and the jock. The comfort, well-being, independence, and fitness of the private man generated building types and ways of dwelling that were inimical to the form of a continuous public townscape.

The second-era town consists mostly of three building types —office parks which constitute the work place, shopping centers which make up the market place, and large residential Planned Unit Developments (PUDs) which provide the dwelling place.

At the typical office park in California, the area of surface parking is four times the footprint of the buildings. In one-story shopping centers the parking area is three times that of the buildings and in two-story shopping centers, up to six times. In residential PUDs parking ranges from half the footprint of the houses to one-and-a-half times. The economics of each of these building types dictates that when land cost or planning law require the use of public transit or double-deckered or underground parking, then developers move to cheaper, less regulated, more remote places, use more land, create sprawl, and perpetuate dependence on the automobile. So what happens to main street and hometown? What happens to the pedestrian and public places? Is all this the workings of an inexorable historic dialectic that we can do nothing about? And, is it really so bad?

There are, I think, five major things wrong with the second-era town.

First: The second-era town wrecks the landscape. The blurred distinction between countryside and town demeans both. In many parts of California there is no longer either countryside or town.

Second: The second-era town devours resources—gasoline, land, air, infrastructure. This is no new story.

Third: As the second-era town becomes less and less convenient, it uses people's time in terrible ways. Life in the land-use map dooms us to hours each day of the vacuous torture of getting from one colored blob to the next.

Fourth: Because it is built in such large chunks, the second-era town discriminates against everyone who is not in a "market sector." The big world of Planned Unit Developments simply does not make odd little corners for people with odd little lives. It is by nature homogenizing and intolerant.

Fifth: Perhaps worst of all, the sanitized anti-urban world of the second era is a place of diminished experience and diminished insight for its inhabitants.

It is significant that the word for the armature of public space in traditional cities is frequently coupled with a word to describe intelligence in the phrase "street-smart." There is no comparable form of suburban wisdom to which one could refer, such as "mall-smart" or "cul-de-sac-smart."

The urban encounters that educate people to become street-smart are confrontations with a full and unedited range of human possibilities which include failure, tragedy, envy, and evil. If one thinks of descriptions of streets in Dickens or Joyce or Virginia Woolf, one thinks of a dense and infinite stream of the particular where the familiar and the unanticipated mingle unpredictably. To experience the immediacy of the particular, one must walk; driving is another experience altogether. And one must walk in places without locks or security guards—in places that are public. The predictable and edited human encounters of the shopping mall, the office park and the condo rec room are to daily life what Club Med is to travel.

If one visits the new places and talks with the planners, architects, developers, traffic engineers, and building officials, it is hard to find anyone who would like to live in the town they are building. If one asks any of these people why they chose to make the place the way they did one generally receives a version of Adolph Eichmann's testimony at the House of Justice in Jerusalem. They all say, "I didn't do it. All I did was my little job. But the whole system is out of the control of individuals like me." Architects are the most vigorous defenders of their own non-culpability; they claim not only individual but collective innocence. "Architects didn't build this town," they say, "it was the developers, the bankers, the traffic engineers; it was the distribution of goods, the lending policy, the electronics industry, the accumulation of capital." But in a weird and corrupted way our patterns of suburbia are as much a triumph of belief as they are a product of circumstance.

The effect of the Usonian house combined with FHA-MPS was to alter at one stroke a two hundred-year legacy of American urbanism, to turn away at one decisive moment from deep and engraved images of the American townscape and to set out on an unknown course. The impulse to do this came not from banks or developers but from architects—not venal or stupid architects but the noblest and most high-minded architects.

By 1960 the banalized plan of Radburn filled with banalized Usonian houses had become such a numbing convention that architects agitated for something new—a new freedom for invention. Architects argued that the setbacks and lot lines of subdivisions wasted land, created sprawl, made dumb little spaces and mindless rows of identical little houses.

Around 1960 there were two major changes in American urbanism. First, the large-scale introduction of the magic marker —what Louis Kahn referred to as "those vulgar pencils that smell like benzene." Second was the advent of the Planned Unit Development and the hegemony of Fisher/Friedman.

In Planned Developments architects are free to push things around, to put dwellings in little clusters, to consolidate gardens and parking areas. Lot lines and streets disappear

Workplace. *Left*
Dwelling. *Right*

altogether, and the last links to the history, structure and continuous fabric of the gridiron town are severed. PUDs have walls around them, and behind the walls, rows of parked cars separate the private fantasy of one developer, architect and marketing team from the next. Magic markers make magic marks. They transformed the landscape of banality of the 1950s into a landscape of metaphor in the '60s: Mariner's Cove, Tonga Gardens, Briar Heath, Broad Sunlit Uplands. If history was the victim of the first generation of post-war development, reality was the victim of the second.

In this new landscape, at one end of the journey from work place to dwelling sits a sealed glass skin building on a lawn with little bumps on it; curving paths, never travelled, wind through the bumps. One enters the building through a parking structure; the spaces inside are made of demountable partitions (originally developed by Skidmore, Owings & Merrill for the Reynolds Metal Building in the 1950s) and are crowned by an acoustic tile ceiling with integrated laylights and HVAC. At lunch one does not leave the building but goes to the canteen, sits in an injection molded Eames chair and eats stuff from a steam table.

At the other end of the journey lies the wall of the PUD, a curving cul-de-sac of continuous garage doors. One walks from the garage directly into a private electronic garden house equipped with VCR, PC, hibachi, hot tub, and nautilus machine.

At the starting gate on one side of the trip stands Mies van der Rohe, Le Corbusier, Konrad Wachsman, and Sasaki/Walker, "out of Olmsted." At the other end—Frank Lloyd Wright, Clarence Stein, Henry Wright, and Richard Neutra. Architects are not such passive bunnies after all.

Over the past dozen years or more, town life and the reconstruction of a public world has become the dominant theme at gatherings such as [the 1988 Pedestrian Pocket symposium at the University of Washington] and in the schools of architecture. If architects hope to instigate the reconstruction of a public world, it should be obvious that this re-creation cannot be a simple rewinding of history. There is no conceivable circumstance in which people will choose to relinquish their sunlight, their privacy, their cars, their fancy bathrooms, their access to the out-of-doors. The institutions of community—the cafe, the street, the porch, the square, the public conveyance—are doomed if they threaten the private man.

Jonas Salk's work in immunology uses the viruses that cause disease to inoculate the patient against the illness. I believe that an architect who wants to help bring about the reincarnation of the public world must master the two forces that killed it—the quest for private comfort and the automobile.

Like every other architect of my generation I am as much the prisoner of the two Clint Eastwood mythologies as anyone else. My work with private houses, housing and town planning is my attempt to build a strategy for the reincarnation of a public world in a society dominated by private values. Private houses are portraits of the most personal aspirations and indulgences of their patrons, and I see them as not peripheral but as central to the bigger job of contributing to a new kind of townscape. Because it is impossible to go backwards in the historical march toward comfort and luxury, private houses contain the irreducible elements, the building blocks of the new town. This town must provide the privacy, comfort, security, sunlight, and access to the land that is contained in the dream of the private house.

In isolated settings a house paradigm can be examined and interpreted without concessions to an urban circumstance. In urban and suburban housing there is a constant struggle to keep the formal conventions and quality of life contained in these house paradigms intact. The private inside and the public outside serve different masters. This dialectic is of sufficient interest to keep one thoroughly absorbed for a lifetime.

David Wyatt has written a remarkable book of essays about the role that California as a setting has played in the imagination of writers. The book is called *Fall into Eden*. In the introduction he paraphrases the California historian Kevin Starr

who Wyatt says considers the story of California to be "the recurring betrayal of a consciously articulated dream."

The contention behind what I have said and shown here is that this poor fellow in San Jose who waters his driveway because there is nothing else left to water has been betrayed. The lady who runs laps in the parking lot of her apartment complex is in hopeless pursuit of an irresistible illusion of private comfort, of mobility and of pastoral bliss. But like the Uroboros, the self-devouring serpent, that illusion has consumed itself.

I hope that the work I have [reproduced] here provides for me and maybe for some others a glimmer of hope that the snake might let go of its tail, that there might be a new path and that in the future our creative acts might not be synonymous with acts of destruction.

[Editor's note: This essay was originally presented as the annual Lionel Pries Lecture at the University of Washington during the charrette in March 1988.]

Pedestrian Pocket Program
AUBURN, WASHINGTON

The general nature and goals of a Pedestrian Pocket have already been described. The following is a guideline for the program of development on the 90-acre site along the Burlington Northern rail line between 277th and 285th streets. This program can and probably will be modified and extended by the different groups, but it should provide a minimum starting point. In addition to developing a master plan for the various uses and configurations of the site, the teams should explore a strategy for the implementation of the Pocket over time. [Pockets can come in three different sizes: quarter, half and full. The current program provides for a "half" Pocket. The program can be sited on either 60 or 90 acres although the 60-acre PP would not have single-family detached houses and the 90-acre PP accommodates additional active and passive open space. For a full-sized PP, of 120–150 acres, this program should essentially be doubled, and for a quarter-sized PP, of 30–45 acres, it should be halved.]

Light Rail Station   10,000 square feet minimum
   Located on the Burlington Northern line in order to provide service to Seattle.
Back Office   500,000 sf
   Back office or office facility for a large corporate tenant with a typical floor plan of at least 40,000 sf and open plan interiors.
Service Office   150,000 sf
   Smaller tenant market spaces of varying square footage, with a minimum of 1,000 sf suites, as is typically found in mixed commercial areas.

Neighborhood Retail Facilities   60,000 sf
   Ground-floor commercial spaces serving residents and
   workers. Sized for the daily population of the Pocket and
   including restaurants, services, stores, markets, and shops.
Commercial Parking   1,000 stalls
   Computed at half the standard requirement in order to encourage transit and carpool use. 700 of the parking stalls
   must be contiguous with the commercial facilities; 300 can
   be peripheral. Structured pairing of two levels is considered
   feasible.
Apartments   400 units
   Designed for individuals or childless couples. Affordable
   two- or three-story flats over parking. Parking requirements
   are two per unit.
Townhouses/Duplexes   400 units
   Two-story units with private yards and attached two car
   garages.
Single Family Detached Houses   50 units
   Small lot family homes with garages on lots of a minimum
   of 3,500 sf.
Elderly Congregate Living Facilities   150 units
   Typically two-story clustered housing with a centrally lo-
   cated community facility. Parking at one stall for four units.
Day-Care Facilities   2 @ 7,500 sf
   Two facilities for 100 children each with four separate ex-
   terior play areas of 3,000 sf each. Elementary and secondary
   schools are assumed to be existing.
Civic Facilities   25,000 sf
   A police station, fire house and Town Hall-type meeting and
   administrative facility with optional churches, post office,
   library, etc.
Parks and Recreational Facilities   12 acres
   A central public area that accommodates activities and features as defined by the sports teams. Does not include open
   areas common to an individual cluster of housing or a commercial complex.

[Editor's note: This program was made available to members of
the four "Pedestrian Pocket" design teams for the workshop of
March 28–April 1, 1988.]

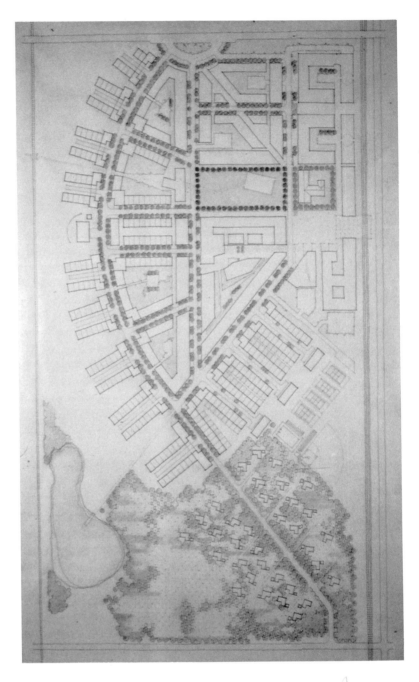

Mack/Prowler

DON PROWLER

In his landmark work *On Growth and Form*, D'Arcy Thompson postulated that organisms have "natural" morphologies and sizes based on the limiting influence of physical forces as expressed by mathematical relationships. While the veracity of his position has been accepted for individual species, we have been reluctant to extend this argument to the aggregations of organisms we call cities. Indeed, if such limits exist for the city, on what are they predicated? Are they based on the number of inhabitants necessary to support a symphony, an airport, a primary school, or a municipal bond? Conceived in an orgy of "auto-eradicism," the Pedestrian Pocket takes the didactic position that the critical limiting factor is the quarter-mile walking radius which maximizes pedestrian access.

Two principle themes inform our team's project for the Pedestrian Pocket charrette: the search for a viable, sustained public realm and the desire to reveal the unique "facilities and difficulties" latent in the site. These two tendencies merge in a concern for the making of discernable places—exterior rooms for public occupation, rooms which are, in some sense, inherent in the site.

"Europe has its cafes," an aphorism contends, "and America its bathrooms." The relative significance of the public and private domain is certainly one of the critical issues in our scheme; we believe that America requires more espresso and less plumbing. Consequently, we seek to sustain a sufficient density of development (at the expense, to some degree, of private space) in order to provide places for spontaneous, informal public gathering throughout the community. High-density residential and mixed-use development allow us to maintain the integrity of the building facade as a boundary for defined streets, block interiors and green spaces of different scales—stages on which the community can play out the small dramas of daily life.

The site plan offers formally differentiated loci within a simple, comprehensible overall pattern. The Mountain View down the Old Post Road, the migration of the scheme to the busy intersection at the northeast corner of the site, the inflection from the freight rail right-of-way at the west edge of the site, and the retention and reuse of the Old Barn (the only object on the site with an "aura," in Walter Benjamin's sense) are all efforts to situate North Auburn Station uniquely on the site—a site devoid of most architectural context.

IN THE BACK OF THE BLOCK

The common open space behind the housing units.

MARK MACK

To look for new viable forms of suburbia or for a quality-oriented conglomeration of housing, commerce and streetscape, we must look at models that have been previously tested.

While the future points to a subdivision that is more developed, market-oriented and decorated in order to satisfy the hunger for prestige and heritage, the past holds some of the models for appropriate solutions. If postmodernism in architecture focuses on the past as an array of forms and images to emulate, postmodern planning must look to models that embody values which enrich and embellish the existence of man and the environment, for the good of the many and not only the few.

For me, the inspiring models for this charrette were products of the housing revolution in northern Germany built, predominantly in Berlin, under the auspices of Martin Wagner and Bruno Taut. Wagner and Taut were concerned with achieving a housing environment that included exterior as well as interior resolutions, connections to transportation and a new interpretation of materialism—i.e. colored stucco—instead of formalism on the facades. As Taut said in 1920, "…instead of the dirty grey houses, finally, the blue, red, yellow, green, black, white houses in uninterrupted shining coloration appears."

NEAR THE FIREHOUSE

A curving residential street accommodating on-street parking.

While the previous epoch had employed apartment build-ings as a typology to reinforce the urban grid or the maximum-density layout of the city, the new housing of Wagner and Taut tried to achieve variety, lower density and an indoor/outdoor relationship with the natural environment.

Looking back to this past, where balanced social, cultural and economic concerns accommodated a quality housing en-vironment, we were inspired to make our mark on the flat and almost featureless site of North Auburn.

Wedged between two railroad stations, our Pedestrian Pock-et strives for a unifying concept to become the mental map of the town and seeks to incorporate the variety of experiences that contribute to the richness of the urban/rural environment.

Further, the emphasis centers around:

- the accessibility, both pedestrian and automobile, of housing and commerce,
- the variety of housing solutions,
- the creation of distinctive places and points of inter-action, especially for pedestrians,
- the hierarchy of building types, including landmarks,

A view of the Lawn Arcade, culminating at Clock Corner. The Old Barn is at left.

• the creation of a binding urban element (i.e., the light standards),

• the retention of a sense of the original place and the natural features of the site (i.e., the pond in the low spot). Radiating (but not radiant) from the (barn) railroad station, the hierarchy of buildings and open spaces unfolds: the main square, the barn, the offices with their underground parking, the commercial quarters with housing for the elderly above (located in close proximity to the railroad station), the day-care labyrinth, the inn on the green, the three-story apartments with parking (with easy access to Main Street), the townhouses and their cul-de-sac entrances on the perimeter, and the single family houses in the orchard.

Street width, planting, interior courts, exterior plazas, and the variety of one- to three-story housing are the building blocks of this scheme. While facades, materials and construction usually contribute greatly to the quality of a particular development, we hope that this pedestrian point of view focuses more or less on a slow transformation from urban sensibilities toward suburban ones. It offers a quality environment through its integration of the outdoor environment and the relatively standardized interiors. As Taut remarked in 1931, "...the immediate exterior environment of the apartment can heighten or lower the quality of living in the apartment."

The idea is from the legacy of European housing experiments. The overall concept is an organization which can be felt. Where is the big street? Where are the landmarks?

MORNING AT NORTH AUBURN STATION *A MODERN FAIRY TALE*

On a day in the near future, the dawn breaks at North Auburn Station. John and Jane Radburn, a young married couple with two children, a dog and a mortgage, are busy in their townhouse just off the Old Post Road near the Fire Station. Jane Radburn is a dedicated, hard-working aerospace engineer who plays a better-than-average game of tennis. John Radburn is a college-educated, dependable, non-union-ized house-husband with a part-time job at the Pocket-Plex office at the station; however, his life revolves primarily around his kids, Jane Jr. and Ronald, who are eight and four years old respectively.

On this morning, the entire Radburn family leaves home together. With the kids in tow, John and Jane head for the Market Square by way of the Lawn Arcade. At Clock Corner, Jane picks up a copy of the Pocket Packet for light rail reading during the five minute trip to her job at the South Auburn Station while John uses the opportunity to bank at the automatic teller.

After distributing kisses to the kids and an errand list to her husband, Jane parts company for the train. The errand list includes a reminder to be at the realtor at half past five for a visit

42

to the new home in the Basque that John and Jane are thinking of purchasing.

John escorts Jane Jr. to her third grade class at the Barn School and deposits Ronald at the day-care center. The center's shape mimics the North Auburn cemetery on the other side of the tracks and confirms that North Auburn Station is a cradle-to-grave community. As always, Old Granny Apple waves to John and Jane Jr. from her window above the Lawn Arcade. Granny Apple loves to beguile John and the kids with stories of her youth with its carefree drives in the country. John makes a mental note to visit Granny later in the week.

At last dependent-less, John walks to Pocket-Plex for his morning stint at the terminal. John enjoys his work, although he would be the first to admit there are times when he finds it less than challenging. Sometimes, as on days like this morning, he daydreams about going back to school—perhaps for an architecture degree. Architecture, John vaguely senses, makes a difference.

[Editor's Note: This fable was discovered along the Way, on the back of a milk carton.]

Student Team: Steve Beck, Christine Berman, Brooke Freeman, Randall Gould, Ben Hansen, Einar Jarmund, Tim Jewett, Jeff Johansen, Eric Kaiser, Tim Matthies, Brian Milne, Steve Nordlund, Stacy Perrigo, Tony Pydych, Kathryn Rogers, Bill Sowles, Susan Whitfield.

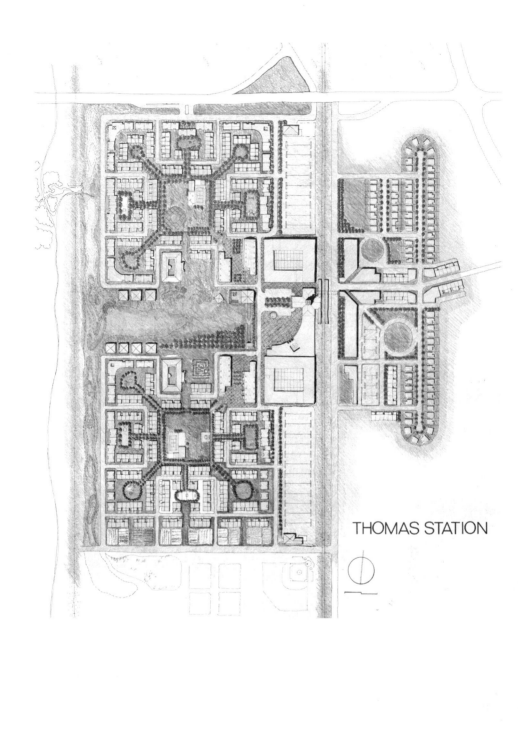

THOMAS STATION

Calthorpe/Kelbaugh

DOUG KELBAUGH

Our scheme was in many ways the least extreme and the most "American." With Peter Calthorpe co-leading the team, we were no doubt the most influenced by the original Pedestrian Pocket diagram, which was developed by Calthorpe in 1988. We asked our students to brainstorm as many ideas as possible so as to generate the largest possible gene pool of ideas on which to draw. After quickly testing some of these ideas (including several that emphasized the diagonal view to Mount Rainier), we settled on modifying the original PP site diagram rather than inventing a new one. In the testing period we examined vehicular circulation, abandoning the peripheral loop for a street grid in the residential sectors. We ultimately returned to the Raburnesque loop road of the original plan,

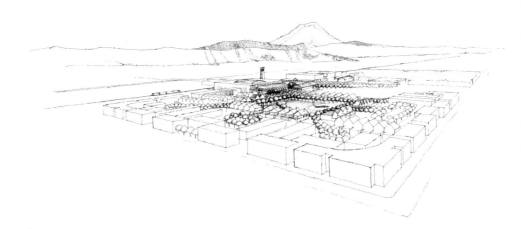

Looking south over the town
center. Perimeter block
housing fills the foreground.

inflecting in this diagram the particularities of the site. Since a
suburban development strategy is nothing else if it's not pedestrian, a clear, safe and rich hierarchy of pedestrian space was
fundamental to our scheme. The creation of variations in size,
configuration and linkage of these recreational, commercial,
civic, garden, and circulation spaces was one of our preoccupa-
tions.

Other notable aspects include the naturalistic berm to the
west which simultaneously blocks noise from the western railroad tracks and provides a sense of visual closure and finite-
ness to the otherwise placeless site. A large green sward, not
unlike an Olmstedian "sheep meadow," connects this berm to
the town center. This park is flanked by gardens, water features
and housing for the elderly and also serves to separate and give
definition to the two "nine-square" residential quarters which
take up the bulk of the site.

The town center focuses on the rail station. The station and
the Town Hall are the only figural buildings in the Pocket, as
befits their civic importance. The large "back offices" straddle
the central plaza. Each has a vaulted atrium to bring more light
and life into what is the least humane building type in the
project. Large tree-filled parking lots to the north and south act
as park-and-ride facilities as well as buffers to the eastern rail
lines. Main Street is three blocks long and is visually closed by
a crook at either end of the street. Along this street lies commercial space with offices above. These four vaulted "market
place" buildings act as urban pedestrian market plazas and link
the housing precincts to the town center.

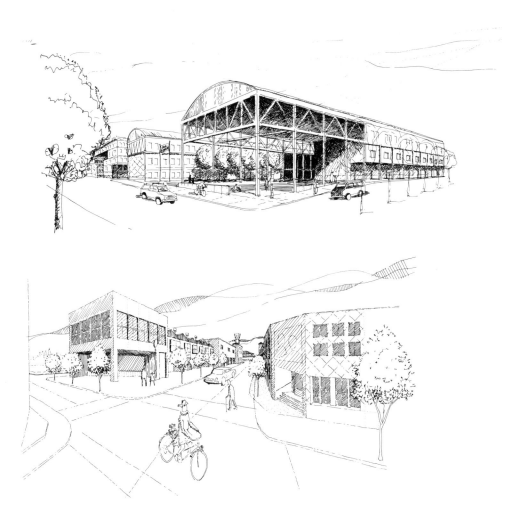

Two of the four vaulted "marketplace" buildings. The diagonals that intersect them serve as pedestrian links between the housing precincts and the town center. *Top* Mixed-use neighborhoods with a variety of building types and conventional streets and sidewalks promote the sort of pedestrian life so essential to healthy, unprogrammed commercial and social interaction. *Bottom*

The police building and firehouse act like lone sentinels next to the vehicular entrances at either end of the Pocket, vegetable gardens and active recreational space flank the southern edge of the site and a tunnel under the railroad tracks preserves the marshlands.

Our scheme actively incorporates the existing suburban housing to the east of the site with the Pocket. The rail station is thus able to serve existing and new housing that is woven into and embroiders the existing suburban fabric. This fuller use of the transit system seems essential to its economic feasibility, on which the success of Pedestrian Pockets so depends.

East elevation of Main Street looking toward the rail station, the only figural/monumental building in the scheme other than the Town Hall. The station faces the Town Hall across Main Street.

PETER CALTHORPE

This scheme is an application of Radburn design principles to the Pedestrian Pocket concept. The Radburn master plan, developed by Stein and Perry in the 1920s, clustered housing around a connected system of open spaces configured into quarter-mile "neighborhoods." In each neighborhood, paths linked a public school and a recreational area to every house. As all front doors opened onto this common green, it became the social center of the neighborhood. The lasting innovations of the plan are the common open space, the dual system for cars and pedestrians, and the complete separation of the automobile from the semi-private open space. The negative aspects of the plan were its inward quality, its disconnection from surrounding towns and the isolation resulting from its limited focus.

The Radburn plan has been loudly discredited for killing the social life of the street by removing the pedestrian, confusing the front and back doors of the house and being a single-use plan. Although some of these criticisms are valid, it must be understood that the suburban context makes many of the same mistakes. The current suburban condition rarely provides mixed-use vitality or socially active neighborhood streets. In an indirect way Radburn is the ancestor of the Planned Unit Development.

The concept of the Pedestrian Pocket corrects and reorients much of what the Radburn plan started. With high-density housing, common open spaces are more critical than with typical low-density suburban types. More significantly, the Pedestrian Pocket extends the destinations of pedestrian paths beyond the Radburn model by arranging retail, mass transit, jobs, entertainment, and recreation within a walkable radius. This mix and the emphasis on walking may not mandate a segregated pedestrian system parallel to the automobile system, but it reinforces the argument for the one that appears here.

In our design, the site is separated into three housing neighborhoods: two high-density clusters—each arranged around a central green, with paths leading to the town center—and a

Student Team: Dan Bollinger, Paul Dorn, Gary Gilbert, Molly Headly, Nora Liu, Heikki Lonka, Ann McBurney, John McLaren, Margaret Menter, Art Peterson, Stephanie Rieken, Pam Root, Shirley Tomita-Geller, Carl Westerback, Diana Wogulis, Mark Wolf.

more typical single-family configuration on the east side of the tracks. A hierarchy of open spaces connects the cluster neighborhoods to the town and the station: private townhouse yards, small cluster commons of twenty to thirty homes, a large two-acre central green with day-care and sports facilities, and a plaza with retail stores and the train station at the town center.

This open space network is surrounded by automobile access to each home in the form of cul-de-sac streets fingering into the neighborhoods. With the segregated pedestrian system, it is possible to walk through the parks to the town center by crossing only one street. The automobile streets form a network connecting homes to common facilities. This dual and redundant system offers choices for many different age groups and trip needs.

The housing itself is configured to place the larger three-story flats at the perimeter of each neighborhood. The two-story townhouses and the units for the elderly are sited along greens, closer to the center in order to provide better access for kids and older people. The distant views therefore are given over to high-density single apartments while the closer landscaping and play areas of the greens are reserved for families.

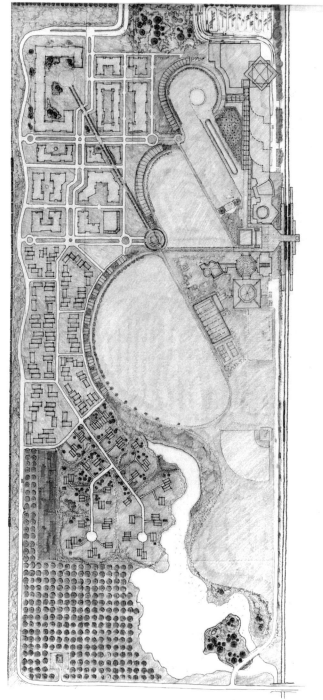

Sellers/Small

DAVID SELLERS

Widespread aimless suburban growth is both the source of new
means of salvaging the development muddle of the entire
United States and the shapeless blob that effortlessly drains
and stagnates the spirit and variety of our expanding culture.
Our team has looked to these suburbs themselves to find an
alternative way of creating communities. The breakdown or
depletion of the system has triggered its own reordering. Ages
ago, Peter Blake (*God's Own Junkyard*) and Louis Mumford (a
film series on automobile strangulation) warned about and ham-
mered on the problems of suburban growth. Yet it is only with
massive commuter tie-ups, relocation of job centers and general
disfunction that the air is cleared for this focus. Appropriate
configurations which last and satisfy human demands are

Looking towards the sports complex, day-care center, library, and town hall.

necessary ingredients for any new settlement landscape; however in this scheme, additional values based on the American dream have been included as essentials.

As an aside, we believe that Romanticization and looking to old Europe is at best an avoidance of inspecting the real issues. No one will argue that the heart jumps in medieval villages and that some basic human needs are bulls-eyed in those old squares, but the malls, elementary/high schools, office parks, and curly 'burban streets offer us clues for our needs in the future. Front porches, bandstands, yard sales, garages, cut-rate stores, a b-ball hoop in the back, the display of the new car or the souping up the old one, lemonade stands, parking lot games, skate boards, and hot-dog biking are some of the new highlights available for designers.

1) A value we suggest in the pedestrian translation of the "burbs" is that there should be a physical change of place between residence and work. There needs to be a meditation or settling time between home and office. (This is accomplished in the car in commuter traffic in typical suburbia.) We have separated housing from shops, schools, and public and commercial functions. This distinction recognizes the commute. We don't honor the beginning and end of the commute: the parking hassle. Nor do we value the extent of time committed to the typical commute. Three to four minutes is enough. In our scheme, one has to walk for several minutes across or along a green park-like space to get from work to home. While walking, the flux of information—air, smells, temperature changes,

seasonal changes, interpersonal opportunities—are valued. Much of the prime time of people's lives in American is spent in isolation, sealed up in cars. The contribution this reality makes to stress and anxiety, divorce and split families is too big a price to pay. In response, the scheme places a premium on being able to drop in at school or go home for lunch or lounge around in the park.

2) The train station should link the anchors, which in this case are the office tower and job center at one end of the galleria and the town hall court (including the town hall, library, day-care facilities, elementary school, and public gym) at the other. The linkage offers the satellites (small shops) between them the best shot at surviving. With this idea, we are integrating a formula that accounts for part of the success of shopping malls. The malls teach that (a minimum of) two anchors are necessary for flow to occur and for the mass (density) of human experience necessary to energize spaces to be generated.

3) There must be resonance and harmony between the physical configuration of the open spaces, views, orientation, and construction details and the site's actual location. This grounding acknowledges climate, local materials, history, geology and any significant aspect of the site. In this site-specific example we have selected alignment with Mt. Rainier for pedestrian pathways and views across the park spaces. The edges of the parks and the lines of housing weave and undulate in a manner reminiscent of the course of the Green River, the long-ago creator of the valley. The notion is that a physical and historical resonance between location and landscape locks in the memory of the place and creates the opportunity for a plurality of individual and collected harmonies.

4) The landscape should be manipulated so that its density is varied. Here, density decreases as one moves from walk-ups at one end of the site to individual suburban houses at the other. With the same concern we have expanded and softened the man-made landscape from controlled gardens to rolling parks to wild ponds and native shrubs. We seek to offer kids, adults and the elderly a full range of common spaces for their use during their discretionary time. Woven within this spatial variety is a number of alternative residential configurations for individuals and families, complete with back alleys, mini-parks and walkways; size and life-style changes do not necessarily mean moving out.

ROBERT SMALL

Our site is a passive plane. Like many sites that may become
available for future Pedestrian Pockets, it is bounded by agricul-
tural/orthogonal gridding. Its configuration is sensitive to transportation systems and non-responsive to natural systems. Our
site is or will become part of an evolving development fabric.
According to the comprehensive plan, it cannot remain buf-
fered by off-site undeveloped open space as this border will
soon be infilled as an industrial park. Moreover, there is a great
need for enlightened land-use advocacy to plan for linkages
and the sharing of open space with the surrounding community
or adjacent Pockets. The Pedestrian Pocket concept, however,
accepts self-containment as the likelihood for most future Pockets. Indeed, in our specific case, this seems to be true. Three of
our four orthogonal edges are almost impenetrable, and the last
is likely to become so. Hence we have the freedom to concen-
trate on enhancing the interior living/work settlement. Access
to the rest of the world is celebrated by a jump on the light rail.

Our site—first forested wetlands and fishing grounds, then a
market truck farm, now a Pedestrian Pocket—is endowed with a
rich and timeless visual prospect, which is probably much more
than most Pocket sites will have. Our basic concept responds to
this prospect. The open space core flows in an undulating, widening course from north to south. At the northern end, a grove of
cedars—the "watershed"—nurtures the headwater in the urban
plaza. The plaza opens to a widening of the parterre. As the cause-

way/promenade that links dwelling to workplace, community amenity and rail station, the parterre merges town with meadow and wetlands. This linear core, like the valley in which it sits, creates the view and foreground for the built forms flanking it. The progressive widening of the core to the south invites sunlight and glimpses of the ephemeral mighty mountain.

The density of the built form decreases when moving from north to south. The plaza and parterre are the active urban meeting grounds between the highest-density dwellings (three- to four-story flats and maisonettes) and the workplace (the back office). The meadow is a more passive meeting ground between low-density attached dwellings (row and town houses) and community services. The wetlands separate the lowest-density houses (zero lot line duplexes) and community recreation.

The dwelling environment—composed of the above mentioned four house types—has a total of one thousand units. Despite the diversity, the modest total does not present the opportunity for heterogeneity; with this in mind, we chose to perpetuate traditional neighborhoods of each type. However, we could not justify introducing the detached single unit—the symbolic American dream house (no matter how "redefined")—into such an intensively developed site. The site carries a housing density much greater than a typical suburb although considerably less than normal urban mid-rise.

To accommodate the generous and varied open spaces, the built forms are clustered closely together. To the west lies the dwelling environment. The farm/orchard and wetlands flank the southern edge of the site to create a vegetative/water view shed and a landmark for the site and micro-region. The back office, parking and retail are consolidated in the northern corner of the eastern section. Civic facilities stand against the southern flank of the east-west causeway while accessing the generous open space of meadow and wetlands on their west and south sides.

Student Team: Janet Breed, Crystal Coleman, Juli Hughes, Mohamed Jasser, Kris Maher, Ted Nash, Debra Springer, Shingo Suekanne, Natnael Tilahun, Ann Tyson, Julie Warrick, Bob Yakas.

The light rail station bridges the two business-oriented sectors. This functional/secular institution is restrained from dominating; it is held in equipoise with dwelling, work and civic institutions. The back-office facilities are housed in a continuous multi-storied built form that cascades down to the northern flank of the light rail station and embraces the promenade/belvedere which foregrounds the retail services. At the other end of the causeway, the educational, day-care and recreational facilities share the internal open space.

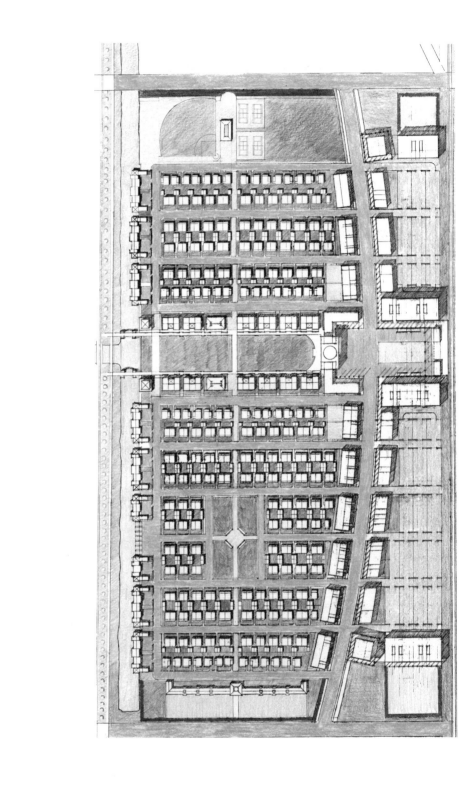

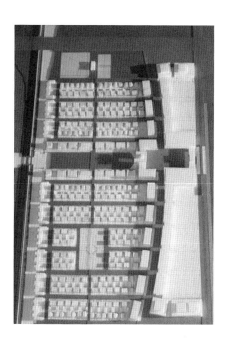

Fraker/Solomon

TASCA PEDONALE

HARRISON FRAKER AND DANIEL SOLOMON

All of the charrette schemes share the good sense and virtues of the Pedestrian Pocket idea, but each is a distinct and different plan type. The Prowler/Mack scheme is like the German *siedlung* plan of the 1920s. The Calthorpe/Kelbaugh plan has its roots in Radburn and the ideas of Clarence Stein and Henry Wright. Sellers/Small take normal contemporary suburban building types and compress them. Our plan is a gridiron based upon the conventions and traditions of the gridiron town. In the Northwest, which has not been completely engulfed by faceless sprawl, the gridiron town and the architecture that goes with it have a sense of familiarity and realness. We believe that the design of the Pedestrian Pocket should strive to avoid the contrived or theme-like artificiality that a self-contained entity could have. Both the architecture and the planning of our "Tasca Pedonale" address this concern.

The main street of Tasca Pedonale connects, at both of its ends, to the country road system and, through this, to highway ramps about a quarter of a mile outside of town. Main Street provides the backbone for Tasca Pedonale. It serves as the automobile entrance, is the principal commercial street and functions as one of the main north-south pedestrian routes. On the eastern side of the street, a continuous row of linked buildings contains two levels of walk-up professional offices and/or retail in a two-story arcade. Above, two-and-a-half stories of residential units are served by a double-height skylit corridor. Bracketed eaves shelter a curbside drop off and support a large trellised porch which buffers the units from parking in the back. The gentle curve of the street creates a handsome serial vista of the arcades and eaves. On the western building, three stories of housing over a partially depressed parking podium animate the pedestrian street. The building type is a hybrid of double-loaded corridor apartments and walk-up flats. The bottom two floors are accessed directly from the street or podium; the upper level is served by an elevator lobby and skylit corridor. Towards the center of the town, these buildings house corner stones in their bases.

An important feature of the plan is the manner in which large areas of inexpensive surface parking are placed immediately next to the retail and office space without gouging holes in the continuous pedestrian fabric of this Pocket. Access to the large parking lots behind the mixed-use buildings on the east side of the street is provided by Main Street. The lower two floors of the mixed-use buildings—offices—are interrupted periodically to provide access to the parking area. The upper floors—housing—span these openings. The organization establishes a continuous street wall with a rhythm of grand portals linking Main Street and the parking lots. Parking serves as an acoustic buffer from the rail system for the Main Street buildings.

At the heart of the scheme, approximately two-thirds of the way along the gently curving Main Street, is the town square. The square is bounded on the east by the light rail train (LRT) station. The north and south sides of the square are defined by back-office buildings. (Half the office space is located on the square while the remainder is situated at the ends of Main

Street; here, the offices create entrances to Tasca Pedonale and gain community visibility.) These buildings have large arcades on the ground floor with major pedestrian approaches to the parking behind. Each building has a stairway that ceremonially overlooks the town square while providing access to the main floor (*piano nobile*) of the back-office space. The west side of the square is defined by the Town Hall complex; from this point, one gets a framed view of the village green, canal, dike, and lake beyond. Town Hall services are located on the first and second floors of the flanking wings, while the town meeting facilities are raised to the third floor in a great room overlooking the town square, the village green, the Green River valley, and Mt. Rainier. The architectural character of the buildings on the town square emerges through the use of heavy timber and masonry construction consistent with guidelines drawn up for the whole development. (See discussion of architectural character below.)

The village green lies directly to the west of the town meeting room. This carefully landscaped open space and lawn is used for strolling and for lawn games such as croquet and bowling on the green. The lawn leads to the canal and the linear park formed by the dike on the opposite bank, with access

AA   BC   AB   BB   CC

Studies of bungalow elevations.

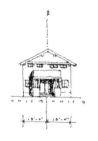

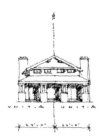

provided by a pair of matching bridges. The dike connects to the Green River two miles to the north. At the end of the axis of the village green, there is a break in the dike, and the railway bridge gives glimpses of a large recreational lake beyond.

Large group houses with apartments for the elderly and single parents line the north and south sides of the green. All of these have front porches facing the green and easy access by back streets to day-care facilities flanking the town hall. The group houses share facilities (kitchen, laundry, recreational ping-pong, pool, cards, etc.) located in two community buildings along the major north-south pedestrian path on either side of the green. An observation pavilion and restaurant/ice cream parlor overlook the canal at the end of the green.

The buildings along the green continue the heavy timber bungalow style of the Town Hall complex but modify this to adjust to their larger scale, creating a relaxed but grand order.

Elements of the residential fabric will be organized by different developers with a common set of design standards establishing relationships of dwellings to streets, locations of parking and the general design character. We have illustrated one potential development scheme. There are three unit types of various sizes designated as plans A, B, and C. The units are paired along party walls to produce six different buildings from the three standard plans: AA, AB, AC, BB, BC, CC. All units have recessed parking served by narrow driveways. Buildings have front porches in the manner of Seattle's great bungalow tradition in order to create a continuous pedestrian fabric for the Pocket.

Important recreational facilities are located at the edges of Tasca Pedonale in order to present a welcoming landscaped transition to the community. Community sports facilities ring the northern edge, and a small field house serves the tennis and basketball courts and baseball and football/soccer fields. The canal, dike and linear park with bike/jogging path create a buffer on the west from the freight rail line. (The canal has special

launching and storage facilities for canoeing.) To the south sits a commercial greenhouse and vegetable farming complex.

A pedestrian path winds its way through the center of the residential streets of Tasca Pedonale, connecting the sports fields, the village green, a residential square with children's playground, and the greenhouse complex, all on a north-south axis. This landscape route provides an alternative to pedestrian circulation along the streets and sidewalks; as a break in the gridiron system, it allows many "short cuts" through the plan.

One of the virtues of American gridiron planning is the sense of location within the landscape that the straight vistas of gridiron streets provide. Seattle and San Francisco, with their continual glimpses of hills and water take advantage of this principle. Tasca Pedonale is planned to give its residents a clear sense of its agrarian setting. Playing fields and allotment gardens terminate north-south views. At the end of the main axis from the rail station, the center square, town hall, and village green, a working dairy farm (Dairy Da) continues the historic agricultural use of the valley and conveys the sense of the town's history. Dairy Da is placed outside the settlement where Deconstruction belongs.

One of the reasons the suburban environment is so dis-jointed is that buildings of disparate typology often have completely different stylistic orientations, despite their physical proximity to each other. For example, slick mirror glass office buildings frequently sit next to shingled vernacular houses

Partial section through center axis of site showing canal and group houses.

with tile-roofed Mediterranean shopping centers nearby. The Pedestrian Pocket compresses the disjunctive quality of suburbia, but by using a common architectural language, it compatibly accommodates all of its mixed uses. In our scheme we have sought this common language in the timber vernacular of the Northwest. Our office and commercial buildings are inspired by the local heavy timber mill and wharf structures, examples of Seattle's high point in the craftsman bungalow tradition.

Phasing for the project will first establish the infrastructure of land forms, streets, utilities, and parking. Construction will begin with the town square and the village green buildings, proceed north and south along Main Street and fill in the residential streets as they correspond to the progress along Main Street. The recreational facilities around the perimeter will be built at the time of the initial infrastructure. Construction will conclude with the canal apartments and the second half of the back-office space.

Tasca Pedonale is organized in a series of layers which run north-south as an analogue to the structure of the valley. The drainage canal with its corresponding dike and linear recreational park not only provides a buffer from the freight train tracks in the west but also makes reference to the hills of the adjacent valley. Similarly the offices and parking on the eastern side of Main Street lessen the noise from the LRT tracks. The drainage canal joins the Green River in the north and introduces Tasca Pedonale to a regional recreation plan. The open space and recreational facilities at the north and south sides provide a green space transition to the local community and give a clear definition to the pedestrian limits of Tasca Pedonale.

Student Team: John Bettman, Paul Chang, Jeff Floor, Jan Fredrickson, Brooke Kelley, Marty Koenigs, Warren Lloyd, Wil Martin, Hikaru Mizumoto, Robin Murphy, Rick Nordby, Stephanie Rieken, Kathy Saunders, Andrew Smith. Todd Tegman, Brock Williams.

The Public Jury
SELECTED COMMENTARY

Audience assembled for the public review. *Top*
Lois Schwenneson, Phil Jacobson. *Middle*
Phil Jacobson, Larry Rouch. *Bottom*

To review the charrette, the University of Washington Department of Architecture assembled a panel consisting of professors of architecture and of urban planning, and County and City of Auburn planners. They were Professor Phil Jacobson, FAIA, Department of Architecture, University of Washington; Mary McCumber of the City of Auburn; Gary Pivo, Department of Urban Design and Planning, University of Washington; Larry Rouch, Architect; Professor Dennis Ryan, Department of Urban Design and Planning, University of Washington; Professor Anne Vernez-Moudon, Department of Planning, University of Washington; and Lois Schwennesen, King County Department of Planning and Economic Development. The discussion took place in front of a large audience of students and public after the presentation of the four charrette schemes by the individual teams.

Dennis Ryan   There's incredible diversity here. What a contrast [between] what could be done versus what is done [in suburbia].

Larry Rouch   There are some strange notions here regarding mobility—mobility as a value unto itself. The issue is rent first of all—rent, later. The issue is control: suburbia is the opportunity to not rub shoulders; urban is where shoulder-rubbing is inevitable. With perhaps the Fraker/Solomon scheme as an exception, the rest all seem intent [upon] recreating the town. [How do these projects] respond to the economic conditions that underlie the suburban landscape?

Phil Jacobson   What about the DESIRE and WILL of the people who are [being] served to demand a solution?...Housing and

employment criteria often don't overlap, but the potential [for] Pedestrian Pockets to be inter-connected and to inter-relate seems exciting. [The several schemes that explore] the perimeter block development idea [which has prompted] German city reconstructions since World War II…make perimeter blocks seem viable.

Gary Pivo   More and more office buildings are being built in the suburbs,…along freeway corridors, usually in one million square foot groupings. It's interesting to consider modifying this existing form of development, but you'll confront an anti-density ethic in the populace [and because of that] in planners as well.

Mary McCumber   What about the regional context? What about all the existing town centers that have problems? Isn't there a certain cavalier-ness inherent in perimeter down-zoning? What about the huge costs of facilities and services?

Anne Vernez-Moudon   It is interesting to see that so many of the teams have used the traditional ways of working cities; there could be a bead of towns. There are some distinct differences in the approach to open space here.

LR   Its interesting to consider land use as a lure for transit; too often you'll hear "You don't have the density yet."

(Comment by Harrison Fraker that perhaps light rail is not to come after but rather to create population density; light rail costs are typically to be "front end" costs.)

LR   Planning decisions are directly connected to legislative decisions.

GP   Consensus organizes growth. Parochial land-use decisions [need to be informed by] regional land-use controls.

MM   You've got to give people choices and design guidance. Communication [of design ideas] might be able to affect land-use valuation.

(Comment by David Sellers: Most people want to have a good life, but their prime time is spent in travel which is part of the reason for high rates of divorce and lost kids. There is a demand for being able to drop by school or go home for lunch. A more holistic approach [allows] more time for our lives.)

LR   What about rent? I see overtures of exclusivity in several of the schemes…[in terms of] socio-economic levels and

Harrison Fraker makes a point. *Top*
Dave Sellers speaks. *Middle*
Team leaders Solomon, Mack, Kelbaugh, Fraker, Calthorpe, and Sellers. *Bottom*

presumed stratification. [For example, contrast Sellers/Small's groupings and Solomon/Fraker's grid.]

DR Today people think that they are getting a choice when all they are usually getting is more waste and more non-economy.

(Comment by Peter Calthorpe: Housing clusters can achieve land affordability; therefore the two-story townhouse type can provide the most amenities at the lowest cost while saving infrastructure costs. Inclusive zoning is a must. Twenty percent of income and time is currently spent on transportation.)

(General comments regarding the impact of two cars per unit parking and the different attitudes to parking expressed by each scheme.)

LR Why is all the recreation arcadian? Maybe recreation[al] differences could be pocket identifiers.

GP Some schemes could make it embarrassing to get into a car....[You can picture] kids walking to stores [and] buying Bazooka bubblegum. It would be nice to see the Pedestrian Pocket concept applied to existing Auburn.

(Comment by Doug Kelbaugh: It's interesting to note how we have an "English" scheme (Sellers/Small), a "German" scheme (Mack/Prowler), an "Italian" scheme (Fraker/Solomon) and an "American" scheme (Calthorpe/Kelbaugh); four suburban types that are loosely based on four different cultures have inadvertently emerged.)

Post-Charrette Review

CHRISTOPHER PERAGINE

The Department of Architecture at the University of Washington was host to an array of distinguished practitioners, assembled by Chairman Doug Kelbaugh, who together with students spent five fruitful, if rainy, days testing the potential of "New Strategies for Suburban Growth: Pedestrian Pockets" proposed by Peter Calthorpe of San Francisco.

In his opening lecture, Calthorpe set forth a formula of mixed-use Main Street and low-rise, high-density housing in a series of 60–120-acre enclaves connected by light rail. Placed at a maximum distance from public transportation of one-quarter mile, the suburban back-office, commercial and residential buildings of Pedestrian Pockets offer an alternative to urban congestion and suburban sprawl. Calthorpe argued that placelessness has become the suburban norm and that suburbanites, separated from the benefits and qualities of an effective public domain, have allowed themselves to become more and more isolated. The sample Pedestrian Pocket program places 1,000 living units with 2,000 to 3,000 residents and an additional 2,000 commuting workers on a 90-acre site. Mass transit links this center (on an existing railroad to be converted to rail transit) to urban centers such as Seattle and Tacoma.

The call to challenge congestion and sprawl with "placemaking" was quickly taken up by student teams led by Harrison Fraker and Dan Solomon, Mark Mack and Don Prowler, David Sellers and Robert Small, and Peter Calthorpe and Doug Kelbaugh. "Let the wild rumpus start," was the cry. That was Monday.

On Tuesday evening, Daniel Solomon presented a galvanizing lecture, maintaining that architects can, and have, made a difference and defending his lavish work for a privileged clientele. His assertion that public interests can be served by elegant private architectural solutions may have been disquieting to some. Solomon's lecture did however offer an unflinching portrayal of the pyrrhic victory of private desires over public virtues in suburbia.

The rain continued. By Thursday it was apparent that the program and the (all too) real site—low-lying, flood-prone, bound by two rail lines, and located on the outskirts of Auburn, Washington, fifteen miles south of Seattle—had generated four very different "solutions." At dawn Friday, the rain momentarily abated, and the work was done. That afternoon and evening the four teams presented the projects to a panel of architecture and urban design faculty and planners from the City of Auburn and the surrounding county.

The Sellers/Small team decided that a site plan that allowed the sinuous and verdant Green River and its open space to extend deeply into the compound, thereby separating the commercial complex from the housing areas, offered the best way to not "leave it go to the zoners." The scheme from the Fraker/Solomon team, with its rigorous street edge and arcades, more closely resembled a traditional nineteenth-century town plan. Their design proposed an architectural strategy that bespoke a curious mix of Italian and Northwest materials and techniques. They adroitly investigated a timber vocabulary that could accommodate both housing and commerce. The Mack/Prowler team's solution was reminiscent of the *siedlung* tradition and was a beguiling presentation of a coherent townscape. Building types that recalled Tessenow's 1920s worker housing schemes offered congregate living; housing for the elderly was sited on a square at the rail station; and a "labyrinth" child-care facility was located at the plan's center. The Calthorpe/Kelbaugh team presented two nine-square neighborhoods separated by a green sward flanked by elderly housing and terminated by the town center. The town center with its figural station/piazza was reached by a hierarchy of "Radburnesque" pedestrian paths.

Since the beginning of the Machine Age there have been many iterations of clustered development, most of which have run against public desire and will. With the Pedestrian Pocket, the point is that we are now in a different era, that the gridlock of our Automotive Age has reached suburbia, and that mass transit and intermittent high-density development are essential for the future well-being of communities. Because the Pockets are contained within a one-quarter mile pedestrian radius, they are considerably smaller and intentionally less ambitious than the New Towns of the 1960s. The question remains whether they will be too modest to survive economically. The week prompted inquiries as to why architects have ceased to play an active role in housing and why such a debilitating gap between architecture and the marketplace has developed. This week-long workshop helped remind everyone that architects can be idealists and advocates capable of helping instigate reconsiderations of how to live.